Vocabulary and Reading Comprehension

Robert Taggart

WALCH PUBLISHING

POWER BASICS

Senior Author . . . . Robert Taggart

Editorial Director . . . . Susan Blair

Project Manager . . . . Mary Rich

Project Editor . . . . Holly Moirs

Director of Marketing . . . . Jeff Taplin

Senior Production Editor . . . . Maggie Jones

Interior Design . . . . Mark Sayer

Cover Design . . . . Roman Laszok

Typesetting . . . . Sheila Russell
Mark Sayer
Ian Weidner

Editorial Staff . . . . Gina Hamilton
Elizabeth Lynch
Richard Lynch
Kate O'Halloran
Erica Varney

3   4   5   6   7   8   9   10
ISBN 0-8251-5553-3
Copyright © 2005
J. Weston Walch, Publisher
P. O. Box 658 • Portland, Maine 04104-0658
walch.com
Printed in the United States of America

WALCH PUBLISHING

Table of Contents

To the Student

Welcome! This *Power Basics*® English/Language Arts book, *Vocabulary and Reading Comprehension,* will help you learn, step by step, how to build your vocabulary and increase reading comprehension. You will learn strategies that will help you understand and remember what you read—for school, for work, for fun, and in everyday life. You will gain useful tools to help you whenever you read, speak, listen, or write.

Unit 1: Vocabulary: Word Parts will teach you about word parts. You will break down long words into shorter parts to see how words are put together. You will increase your vocabulary in two ways. You will learn new vocabulary words in this book. You will also practice applying your knowledge of word parts to unfamiliar words. These skills will help you figure out new words you meet in your reading.

Unit 2: Building Vocabulary will teach you other ways to increase your word power. You will learn about synonyms and antonyms and how these can build your vocabulary. Context clues are important tools in uncovering word meanings. You will use these strategies to learn new words in this book and new words in your reading.

Unit 3: Dictionary Skills will teach you how to use a dictionary to find definitions. It will also help you decide which definition in a list to choose. Through applying and practicing these dictionary skills, you will master another tool for vocabulary-building.

To the Student, *continued*

Unit 4: Understanding What You Read will give you helpful tools to understand what you read. You will learn to "read between the lines" to get more from your reading. You will learn to think about a reading passage while absorbing information. The step-by-step reading process can be applied to any reading you do.

Unit 5: Finding Information in a Passage will teach you how to find information quickly when you do not have time to read a whole passage. This useful skill will help you find review material for tests in textbooks, help you decide if a reference book holds the information you need, and help you find key information in any book or document you read.

Unit 6: Analyzing What You Read will teach you about what lies behind what you read. You will learn about the author's purpose and about writing styles. This will help you form your own opinion about the value of a written piece.

Unit 7: Remembering What You Read will teach you how to remember the information you have gathered from your reading. You will practice thinking critically about what you read and making decisions about it. These valuable strategies will help you prepare for tests and give you reference tools for any reading you do.

UNIT 1

Vocabulary: Word Parts

LESSON 1: Base Words

 GOAL: To learn new vocabulary words by breaking long words into base words

WORDS TO KNOW

base word   compound word

Compound Words

Words are made up of different parts. A base word is one kind of word part. Base words are words that form the main part of a longer word.

Some words are made up of two base words put together. These are compound words. Look at this compound word:

homework

The word *homework* is a compound word. It is made up of the words *home* and *work.*

Now look at this compound word:

sunlight

Do you see the two base words? They are *sun* and *light.*

■ PRACTICE 1: Compound Words

Write the two base words you find in each compound word.

1. speechwriter   _____   _____

2. aftertaste   _____   _____

3. grapevine   _____   _____

4. scoreboard _____ _____

5. skyscraper _____ _____

6. spotlight _____ _____

7. peacekeeper _____ _____

8. stopwatch _____ _____

9. timeworn _____ _____

10. windshield _____ _____

Meanings of Compound Words

You know that a compound word is made up of two base words. The meaning of the compound word combines the meanings of the two base words.

Compound words can be long and seem hard. If you can break the compound word into two shorter words, though, you can figure out the meaning of the longer word.

Look at the following example:

beekeeper

The word above is long and looks odd—it has a lot of *e*'s in a row. If you look closely, however, you see two words: *bee* and *keeper.* Those words aren't so hard. A beekeeper is someone who keeps, or raises, bees. (A beekeeper raises bees for their honey.)

■ PRACTICE 2: Meanings of Compound Words

Read the compound words. Based on the meanings of the base words, write the definition of each compound word.

1. speechwriter _____

_____

2. aftertaste _____

_____

3. grapevine _____

_____

4. scoreboard _____

_____

5. skyscraper _____

_____

6. spotlight _____

_____

7. peacekeeper _____

_____

8. stopwatch _____

_____

9. timeworn _____

_____

10. windshield_____

_____

Base Words

Words are made up of different parts. As you have seen, one kind of word part is called a *base word*. Two base words together make a compound word.

Sometimes base words are joined with other word parts. Look at these examples:

> power<u>ful</u>

> <u>dis</u>pleas<u>ed</u>

The base word in each example is underlined. Other word parts have been added to each base word to form a longer word.

TIP

The entire base word is not always spelled out in the longer word. Look at an example: *celebration.* Can you find the base word? It is *celebrate.* Notice that the final *e* in the base word *celebrate* does not appear in *celebration.* But you can easily find the base word in the longer word.

■ PRACTICE 3: Base Words

Look at the words below. Write the base word of each vocabulary word.

1. purify   _____

2. disconnect   _____

3. falsely   _____

4. employer   _____

5. rewrite   _____

6. readiness   _____

7. misunderstand   _____

8. illegal   _____

9. imprison   _____

10. preheat   _____

11. admirable   _____

12. exploration   _____

13. dangerous   _____

14. fearless   _____

15. punishment   _____

LESSON 2: Prefixes

 GOAL: To learn the meanings of prefixes to understand new words

WORD TO KNOW
prefix

Prefixes

Prefixes are word parts added to the beginning of a word to make a new word. You saw some prefixes when you were working with base words. Look at these examples of words with prefixes:

disconnect   reconnect

The first word, *disconnect,* means to "pull apart" things that are connected. *Disconnect* is the opposite of *connect. Reconnect* means to take something that is disconnected and "connect it again."

As you can see, prefixes can change the meaning of a word a lot!

■ PRACTICE 4: Prefixes
Underline the prefix in each word.

1. disorder
2. reapply
3. misfit
4. tricolor
5. illegal

Prefixes with Number Meanings

Some common prefixes add number meanings to words. Think about a familiar word: *bicycle.* How many wheels does this kind of cycle have? Two. *Bi-* means "two."

Here are some common prefixes with number meanings:

Prefix	Meaning
uni-	one
bi-	two
tri-	three
semi-	half

■ PRACTICE 5: Prefixes with Number Meanings

Write the correct word from the box on the line.

biweekly	semicircle	tricolor	uniform

1. France has a _____ flag. It has blue, white, and red stripes.
2. I am paid _____. I get a check every two weeks.
3. My _____ was blue pants and a white shirt. There was only one choice of what to wear!
4. The children sat in a _____ to hear the story. They could all see the pictures that way.

Prefixes with Time Meanings

Prefixes can sometimes tell when things happen in relation to other things. Here are some prefixes with time meanings:

Prefix	Meaning
pre-	before
post-	after
re-	again

PRACTICE 6: Prefixes with Time Meanings

Read the words in the box. Decide what each word means. Write the word next to its meaning.

postoperative	preschool	rearrange
postwar	preheat	rewrite

1. to write again _____
2. something that happens after a war _____
3. where children too young for school learn _____
4. to arrange again _____
5. to heat before doing something _____
6. something done after an operation _____

TIP

Sometimes a word starts with the letters of a prefix, but they are not a prefix. For example, the *re* in *realize* is not a prefix. In this case, *re* is part of the base word *real.* Look for prefixes, but do not assume that the beginning of every word is a prefix.

Prefixes with Spatial Meanings

Some prefixes tell where things are in relation to other things. These prefixes tell how things are arranged in space. Here are some prefixes with spatial meanings:

Prefix	Meaning
inter-	between
intra-	within
sub-	below, under
super-	over, above
trans-	across, beyond, through

■ PRACTICE 7: Prefixes with Spatial Meanings

Write the correct word from the box on the line.

extraordinary	intraoffice	superpower
international	subtitle	transatlantic

1. The _____ memo was sent to every worker in that office.

2. The _____ was printed below the main title.

3. The _____ agreement was signed by three nations.

4. Charles Lindbergh made the first solo _____ airplane flight in 1927.

5. A(n) _____ is a country that has more power than other countries.

6. Her talent is _____. She can beat all her classmates!

TIP

Sometimes you may run into a word that has a prefix that you recognize but whose meaning you can't remember. Try thinking of a word you know with the same prefix, such as *transportation* for *trans-*. Think of what the familiar word means. For example, *transportation* means "something that carries you across land, sea, or air." Then see if you can use part of that meaning in the new word. Chances are, you'll get close to the correct meaning of the new word.

Prefixes That Make Opposite Meanings

There are many prefixes that create opposite meanings. Here are some prefixes that mean "not" or "the opposite of":

in-	il-	de-	non-
im-	ir-	dis-	un-

TIP

The prefixes *il-, im-,* and *ir-* are all forms of the prefix *in-*. These prefixes are used depending on the spelling of the word to which they are added. For example, *il-* appears in *illegal, im-* is found in *immodest,* and *ir-* is seen in *irresponsible.* Do you see a pattern?

■ PRACTICE 8: Prefixes That Make Opposite Meanings

Add a prefix to each bold word below to make an opposite meaning.

1. Everyone has fear of the _____**known.**
2. We _____**agree** about the music. I want to play rock, but he wants to play hip-hop.
3. The _____**mature** boys laughed at silly jokes.
4. The criminal was _____**sane.** The judge sent him to a hospital.
5. The poem uses _____**sense** words. They do not make sense.
6. Her actions were _____**legal.** She was arrested.
7. She was not old enough yet to take care of her brother. She was _____**responsible.**
8. The computer program does not work. She will _____**bug** it.

Another Meaning of *in-*

The prefixes *in-* and *im-* are very common. They can make a word into its opposite.

The prefixes *in-* and *im-* and the related prefixes *en-* and *em-* have another meaning, too. They can mean "in," or "on." They can change a word to show that something is moving to or being put on or in something else. For example, *imprison* means "to put in prison." To *empower* someone is to put power into him or her.

■ PRACTICE 9: Another Meaning of *in-*
Write the correct word from the box on the line.

embalm	enlarge	enrage	imprint	ingrown

1. The town will _____ the road to take more cars.

2. We will _____ the front cover with the logo.

3. The _____ toenail made it hard to walk.

4. Ancient Egyptians used to _____ bodies with special fluids made of spices.

5. The loss will _____ the fans.

Prefixes with Negative Meanings

Some prefixes change the meaning of a word to the meaning that something is wrong, incorrect, or bad. Here are two prefixes with negative meanings:

     mal-   mis-

■ PRACTICE 10: Prefixes with Negative Meanings

Write the correct word from the box on the line.

malnutrition	misjudge	misunderstand

1. The child had _____. He did not get enough nutrition from his food.
2. I'm afraid he will _____ me. He does not speak much English.
3. Some people _____ him because he wears odd clothes. They do not know what he is really like.

The Prefix ex-

The prefix ex- usually means "former," "formerly," or "no longer." It means that something used to be the case but no longer is.

> **! TIP**
> There is usually a hyphen between the prefix ex- and the base word: *ex-astronaut, ex-student.*

■ PRACTICE 11: The Prefix ex-

Write a word with the prefix ex- that makes sense.

1. The _____ no longer taught. She sometimes filled in if a teacher was sick, though.
2. Rudy is her _____ . Her new husband is Douglas.
3. He is an _____ . He can no longer sing.

> **! TIP**
> An easy way to remember what the prefix ex- means is to think of the letter it sounds like: *x.* The letter *x* is often used to cross something out. When you add the prefix ex- to a base word, you are showing that the base word is no longer true.

LESSON 3: Suffixes

WORD TO KNOW

suffix

Suffixes

You have learned that prefixes are word parts added at the beginning of a word to make a new word. Suffixes are word parts added at the end of a word to make a new word. Look at these examples of words with suffixes:

powerful   powerless

Powerful means "full of power." *Powerless* means the opposite: "having no power." Just like prefixes, suffixes can change a word's meaning in big ways.

When you add suffixes to base words, there are often spelling changes in the root word. Here are some examples:

1. When a suffix is added to a base word that ends in *y*, the *y* is usually changed to *i*. Then the suffix is added. Example: *glory + -ous* —➤ *glorious*

2. Sometimes, the *y* is dropped, then the suffix is added. Example: *memory + -ize* —➤ *memorize*

3. When a base word ends in a vowel, the vowel is often dropped. Then the suffix is added. Example: *culture + -al* —➤ *cultural*

Sometimes, the spelling of a base word may change in other ways. Usually the changes are very small, so you will still see the base word. In the word *wondrous* for example, which means "full of wonder," you can find *wonder* even though the *e* has been dropped.

■ PRACTICE 12: Suffixes

Underline the suffix in each word.

1. graceful

2. darken

3. childish

4. darkness

5. darkly

6. glorify

The Verb Suffixes *-en, -ify,* and *-ize*

Some suffixes can change a word from one type of word to another. The suffixes *-en, -ify,* and *-ize* make words into verbs, or action words. These suffixes mean "to make," "to cause to be," or "to become." Here are some examples of words with these suffixes:

darken	purify	memorize
harden	solidify	tenderize

The suffix *-en* can also mean "made of." For example, a wooden boat is a boat made of wood.

■ PRACTICE 13: The Verb Suffixes *-en, -ify,* and *-ize*

Write the meaning of each word. Use what you know about suffixes to help you.

1. darken _____

2. harden _____

3. purify _____

4. solidify _____

5. memorize _____

6. tenderize _____

The Adjective Suffixes *-ic, -al,* and *-ical*

Some suffixes make base words into adjectives. Adjectives are describing words. For example, someone who is athletic has the physical ability of an athlete. The word *athletic* describes a person with physical talent. The word *musical* describes something that sounds nice, like music. The word *historical* describes something that is important in history.

■ PRACTICE 14: The Adjective Suffixes *-ic, -al,* and *-ical*

Write the meaning of each word. Use what you know about suffixes to help you.

1. educational _____

2. heroic _____

3. spherical _____

The Adjective Suffixes *-ous, -y, -ful,* and *-less*

The suffixes *-ous, -y,* and *-ful* all make adjectives, or describing words, that mean "full of" or "like" something else. For example, a mysterious stranger is full of mystery. A squeaky chair is full of squeaks. A powerful engine is full of power.

The suffix *-less* is the opposite of the suffix *-ful*. It means "being without" or "having none" of something. A hopeless person has no hope.

■ PRACTICE 15: The Adjective Suffixes *-ous, -y, -ful,* and *-less*

Write the meaning of each word. Use what you know about suffixes to help you.

1. hairy _____

2. respectful _____

3. dangerous _____

4. hairless _____

The Adjective Suffixes *-able* and *-ible*

Two common suffixes are *-able* and *-ible*. These suffixes make words that describe something that is able to do something. For example, if someone is dependable, you can depend on him or her.

■ Practice 16: The Adjective Suffixes *-able* and *-ible*

Write the meaning of each word. Use what you know about suffixes to help you.

1. recyclable _____

2. collapsible _____

3. preventable _____

The Suffix -ly

The suffix -ly is very common. It makes adverbs, or words that describe actions. This suffix is added to a base word to tell how something is done. For example, if someone speaks angrily, she or he speaks in an angry way.

The suffix -ly can also mean "happening every (period of time)." For example, a daily walk is a walk you take every day.

■ PRACTICE 17: The Suffix -ly

Write the meaning of each word. Use what you know about suffixes to help you.

1. strangely _____

2. swiftly _____

3. weekly _____

4. weakly _____

The Noun Suffixes -ance and -ence, -hood, -ment, -ness, and -ship

These suffixes carry the meaning "the state of, act of, or condition of being."

-ance	-hood	-ness
-ence	-ment	-ship

These suffixes make nouns, or naming words. For example, the word *difference* means "the condition of being different" from something else. Another meaning of these suffixes is "the act of." A *disturbance* is an act of disturbing someone.

■ PRACTICE 18: The Noun Suffixes *-ance* and *-ence*, *-hood, -ment, -ness,* and *-ship*

Write the meaning of each word. Use what you know about suffixes to help you.

1. occurrence _____

2. attendance _____

3. neighborhood _____

4. placement _____

5. readiness_____

6. ownership _____

The Noun Suffixes *-ion, -tion,* and *-ation*

The suffixes *-ion, -tion,* and *-ation* change action words into nouns. These suffixes can mean "the condition of," "the act of," or "the state of." They can also mean "the way to" do something. For example, to *inform* someone means to tell him something. You can also say that you give him *information.* The way you inform someone is by giving him information.

■ PRACTICE 19: The Noun Suffixes *-ion, -tion,* and *-ation*

Write the meaning of each word. Use what you know about suffixes to help you.

1. confusion _____

2. exploration _____

3. direction _____

Suffixes That Describe People

There are many suffixes that describe people. These suffixes change a word to tell what someone does or where someone is from. Here are some examples:

Suffix	Example	Meaning of Word
-ant	assistant	a person who assists another
-ent	student	a person who studies
-er	runner	a person who runs
-or	visitor	a person who is visiting
-an	musician	a person who makes music
-ian	Canadian	a person who is from Canada
-ist	artist	a person who makes art

■ PRACTICE 20: Suffixes That Describe People

Write the meaning of each word. Use what you know about suffixes to help you.

1. photographer _____

2. tourist _____

3. writer _____

4. hairstylist _____

5. servant _____

LESSON 4: Roots

WORD TO KNOW

root

Roots

You have learned that different word parts combine to make words. Base words, prefixes, and suffixes are all word parts. Roots are another type of word part.

English roots often come from Latin or Greek words. Like a base word, a root is a word part used as the foundation for making other words. Unlike base words, roots are not always stand-alone words themselves. Recognizing and understanding common roots can help you figure out the meaning of new words. Look at this example:

incredible

The root of *incredible* is *cred,* which means "believe." Adding the prefix *in-* and the suffix *-ible* to the root *cred* gives *incredible,* which means "not able to be believed."

SOME COMMON ROOTS

Root	Meaning	Examples
bi, bio	life	biology
cede, ceed, cess	go; yield	concede, exceed, process
cred	believe	incredible
dic, dict	say	dedicate, dictate
duce, duct	lead	induce, conduct

Root	Meaning	Examples
fact, fect, fict, feit	make; do	factory, fiction, perfect, counterfeit
fer	carry	transfer
ject	throw	eject
junct	join	junction
mit, mis	send	remit, mission
pone, pose	place, put	postpone, impose
port	carry	portable
scrib, scrip	write	describe, postscript
secu, sequ	follow	consecutive, sequel
vene, vent	come	convene, prevent
vers, vert	turn	reverse, convert
voc, voke	call	vocal, revoke

■ PRACTICE 21: Roots

Underline the root of each word. (Do not confuse the root with a prefix or a suffix.)

1. transfer

2. mission

3. incredible

4. impose

5. prescription

6. precede

7. inject

8. portable

9. sequence

10. biosphere

■ PRACTICE 22: Meanings of Words with Roots

Write what you think each word means. Use what you know about roots, prefixes, and suffixes.

1. transfer _____

2. mission _____

3. incredible _____

4. impose _____

5. prescription _____

6. precede _____

7. inject _____

8. portable _____

9. sequence _____

10. biosphere _____

IN REAL LIFE

Sometimes you come across hard words on important documents. Look at these words that you might find on a job application:

availability   employment history

qualifications   references

What do you think each word or phrase means? Write your definitions on a separate sheet of paper. Use what you know about word parts to help you.

UNIT 1 REVIEW

Read each word. Circle the letter of the correct definition. Use what you know about word parts to help you.

1. doorstop
   a. something that keeps a door from moving
   b. something that opens a door
   c. a secret entrance

2. watchtower
   a. a tall building
   b. a device to tell time
   c. a tall building from which a person keeps watch

3. disorder
   a. a state of perfect order
   b. a state of no order
   c. to order again

4. repaint
   a. to paint again
   b. to take the paint off
   c. to paint poorly

5. uncertain
   a. quite sure   b. not sure   c. sure

6. worthless
   a. having great value
   b. having a little value
   c. having no value

7. solidify
   a. to melt   b. to make into a gas   c. to make firm

8. endanger
   - **a.** to put in danger
   - **b.** to save from danger
   - **c.** to worry about danger

9. transmit
   - **a.** to walk across something
   - **b.** to send across something
   - **c.** to yell from far away

10. postpone
   - **a.** to push through
   - **b.** to put off until a later time
   - **c.** to place before something else

UNIT 1 APPLICATION ACTIVITY
From Old to New

Look at the front page of a newspaper. Choose four familiar words. Write them on the lines labeled "Word" below. Then create as many new words as you can from each word. Make compound words, or add prefixes or suffixes. Write the new words on another sheet of paper.

Word: _____

Word: _____

Word: _____

Word: _____

UNIT 2
Building Vocabulary

LESSON 5: Synonyms and Antonyms

> **GOAL:** To build vocabulary by learning synonyms and antonyms of words

WORDS TO KNOW

antonym   synonym

Synonyms

One way to build your vocabulary is to learn synonyms for words. Synonyms are words that mean almost the same thing. For example, *joy* is a synonym of *happiness.*

Read the following sentences.

> Rosie shed tears of <u>happiness</u> when she saw all her friends around the table. They wished her <u>happiness</u> on her birthday. Long after the candles were blown out, she would remember the <u>happiness</u> she felt on this day.

Instead of always using *happiness,* the author could have used synonyms, such as *joy, gladness,* or *bliss.* Learning synonyms when you learn a new word builds your vocabulary fast!

TIP

Most synonyms do not have exactly the same meaning. They have nearly the same meaning. Look at these examples:

Mr. Sanjay was furious at his friend.
Mr. Sanjay was angry at his friend.

The words *furious* and *angry* are synonyms, but their meanings are a bit different. *Furious* is stronger than *angry. Furious* means "very angry." Be careful when you choose synonyms. Be sure you are saying what you really want to say!

Think about an activity you enjoy, maybe a sport or a hobby. Do you use a special vocabulary for that activity? For example, if you like to ski, you may use words such as *snow, powder, hardpack,* and *crust.* Do these words mean exactly the same thing? Do you think people who do not ski would know the difference? Do you think any synonyms are ever exactly the same? Write your ideas on another sheet of paper.

⬛ PRACTICE 23: Synonyms

Replace each underlined word on the next page with a synonym from the box. Write the synonym on the line. Remember, synonyms mean almost the same thing.

> aid—to help; to assist
> decipher—to understand; to figure out; to decode
> essential—needed; necessary; vital; required
> furious—very angry
> gigantic—huge, like a giant
> haggard—tired and worn
> humorous—funny; amusing
> intelligent—smart; bright
> liberty—freedom
> option—choice
> outstanding—remarkable; excellent; above average
> peak—summit; high point
> rival—enemy; foe; opponent
> task—job; chore
> tedious—dull; boring

1. Nita was <u>angry</u> with Jim because he forgot her birthday.

   _____

2. She has the <u>freedom</u> to come and go when she wants.

   _____

3. Darnell tried to <u>help</u> the hurt man. _____

4. Petra's first <u>job</u> of the day was to check her e-mail.

   _____

5. Lewis did not find the mean cartoon at all <u>funny</u>.

   _____

6. Alana did an <u>excellent</u> job on her project. _____

7. Emmanuel is a very <u>smart</u> little boy. _____

8. The <u>huge</u> dog scared the children. _____

9. The winning goal was the <u>top</u> of Eric's sports career.

   _____

10. His <u>enemy</u> in the race was a senior. _____

11. We tried to <u>decode</u> the directions. They were not very clear!

    _____

12. It was <u>necessary</u> to find freshwater if we were to live.

    _____

13. We were yawning after two hours of the <u>boring</u> work.

    _____

14. We had only one <u>choice</u> when the car broke down: walk home. _____

15. The woman looked <u>tired</u> after she worked a double shift.

    _____

Antonyms

As you have seen, one way to build your vocabulary is to learn synonyms. Another way is to learn antonyms, or opposites, of words.

Look at the following sentences:

Reggie should have been <u>rested</u> from his vacation. Instead, he looked <u>haggard</u> after his long flight.

<u>Fresh</u> smiles broke out on the <u>haggard</u> faces of the travelers. They had finally landed!

These sentences show how antonyms can show contrast, or differences. Because they are opposites, antonyms are useful for talking about differences between people, things, or ideas (*rested* versus *haggard*). Antonyms can also show when a major change takes place (*haggard faces* to *fresh smiles*).

> **TIP**
>
>
>
> Here is an easy way to remember the difference between synonyms and antonyms. *Synonym* and *similar* begin with the same sound. This can help you remember that synonyms are similar in meaning.

■ PRACTICE 24: Antonyms

Replace each underlined word on the next page with its antonym from the box. Write the antonym on the line.

abandon—to leave behind; to desert
ally—friend
amusing—funny; humorous
complex—hard to solve or separate; complicated
condemned—doomed; criticized
fabulous—great; wonderful
forbid—to not allow; to prohibit
joy—happiness; gladness; bliss
rage—fierce anger
summit—the top point; the peak

1. Haley decided to <u>claim</u> her date. She went home with a friend. _____

2. When the hikers reached the <u>bottom</u>, they planted a flag. _____

3. The <u>bad</u> meal included five courses. _____

4. The <u>serious</u> story made everyone laugh. _____

5. The crowd clapped with <u>sadness</u>. Their side had won! _____

6. She was his <u>enemy</u> at the office. She told him what his boss had said. _____

7. The judge was <u>praised</u> for his decision. It seemed unfair. _____

8. His <u>happiness</u> was clear. He shouted and banged his fist on the table. _____

9. I <u>allow</u> that kind of talk in the classroom. _____

10. The math problem was tricky. It was more <u>simple</u> than I had thought. _____

LESSON 6: Context Clues

GOAL: To learn to use context clues to figure out the meanings of new words

WORDS TO KNOW

context	description	explanation
definition	example	restatement

Context

You know how to look inside a word and use the parts to figure out the word's meaning. You can also look beyond a word to figure out what it means. This is called using context clues.

The **context** of a word is the information surrounding the word. Read the following sentence. Pay attention to the underlined word.

> The whole class laughed at the <u>amusing</u> joke the teacher made.

As you read the sentence above, you probably knew what *amusing* meant without even thinking about it. The context told you that the joke the teacher made was funny. Even if you did not know what the word *amusing* meant, the rest of the sentence would help you understand the word's meaning. The words *laughed* and *joke* describe something funny. *Amusing* was used to describe the word *joke,* so you could also figure out that *amusing* would probably have to do with something funny.

!

Context clues are everywhere! If you come to an unfamiliar word, check out the words just before and just after the new word. If there is a series of words, they may be related. Knowing this can help you figure out the meaning of the unfamiliar word. Look at this example:

His boring speech was <u>monotonous</u> and unexciting.

You can guess the meaning of the word *monotonous* by knowing what *boring* and *unexciting* mean.

■ PRACTICE 25: Context

Read the sentences. Use the context of each sentence to help you figure out what the underlined words mean. Circle the letter of your answer.

1. People under seventeen were <u>prohibited from</u> viewing the violent film.

   a. allowed   **b.** not allowed to   **c.** required to

2. Animals <u>thrive</u> in a zoo that is like their natural home.

   a. do poorly   **b.** die   **c.** do well

3. The <u>itinerary</u> included stops at a museum, an old mill, and a famous restaurant.

   a. plan of events   **b.** map of an area   **c.** bus

Have you ever heard the expression "taken out of context"? The expression is used when someone says something and those words are repeated—without the surrounding context. The words may appear to mean something else if the background information is gone. Look at this example:

I will not raise taxes!

This could be a quotation from any politician. And the sentence may come back to haunt him or her later. Suppose the context of the sentence was "This has been a difficult year for the economy. Many people have lost jobs. This year, I will not raise taxes." Without the context, people might take the words "I will not raise taxes" to mean that the official will never raise taxes. They might accuse the person later of going back on a promise if taxes are ever raised.

It is important to look at the context of what you read and hear. If something sounds unlike what you would expect, be sure your information contains the context.

■ Using Context Clues

There are several types of context clues. Look for these when you come across an unfamiliar word that you cannot break down into smaller parts. A list of types of context clues appears on the next page.

Types of context clues:

restatement—restating a word; giving the meaning by using another group of words in its place

definition—defining a word in the text; giving the word's meaning

synonyms/antonyms—using a known synonym or antonym

description—describing what a word means

explanation—explaining what a word means

examples—giving examples to make the meaning clear

■ PRACTICE 26: Using Context Clues

Read the following paragraphs. Look for context clues to help you understand the underlined words.

Volcanoes

A <u>volcano</u> is an opening in the earth's <u>crust</u>, or outer layer, through which <u>liquid</u> rock and iron is pushed to the surface. This <u>molten</u> rock and iron is called <u>lava</u>. Heat builds up inside the earth. This causes pressure. When the pressure is strong enough, it pushes the lava through the volcano. This release is a volcanic <u>eruption</u>.

An eruption often begins with a huge explosion. Then rivers of lava flow from the volcano. Sometimes steam and other <u>vapors</u>, or gases, are released as well. Volcanoes also <u>expel</u> ash and dust, which blanket the <u>surrounding</u> area. Besides affecting the area around the volcano, an eruption can affect areas far away. Ash enters the <u>atmosphere</u>—the layer of gas around the earth—and affects weather in distant places.

Throughout history, there have been many cases of volcanic eruptions destroying cities. The city of Pompeii was one such city. It was buried under nine feet of ash. Although the eruption of Mt. Vesuvius <u>destroyed</u> the lives of the people living in Pompeii at the time, it <u>preserved</u> history for future people. Whole houses were buried and stayed just as they were at the time of the eruption.

Today, scientists have tools to <u>predict</u> eruptions and can warn people to leave the area before it is too late.

Now answer the questions about the underlined words in the article. Circle the letter of the best answer.

1. Which of the following is a synonym for *liquid*?
   a. molten
   b. volcano
   c. pressure
   d. lava

2. Which of the following is a restatement of *crust*?
   a. volcanic eruption
   b. volcano
   c. molten
   d. outer layer

3. What is another word for *vapors*?
   a. lava
   b. eruption
   c. gases
   d. expel

4. Which phrase restates the meaning of the word *surrounding*?
   a. . . . great amount of ash and dust that blanket the surrounding area.
   b. Besides affecting the area around the volcano . . .
   c. . . . there have been many cases of volcanic eruptions destroying entire cities.
   d. . . . it preserved history for future people.

5. What is a synonym for the word *expel*?
- **a.** release
- **c.** eruption
- **b.** exerted
- **d.** destroying

6. What is the definition of *atmosphere*?
- **a.** a volcanic eruption
- **c.** the earth's outer layer
- **b.** the layer of gas around the earth
- **d.** molten rock and iron

7. Fill in the blank: The first paragraph _____ a volcanic eruption.
- **a.** gives a synonym for
- **c.** defines
- **b.** gives an antonym for
- **d.** explains

8. Which pair of words is an example of using synonyms?
- **a.** vapors/gases
- **c.** volcano/eruption
- **b.** molten/lava
- **d.** destroyed/preserved

9. Which pair of words is an example of using antonyms?
- **a.** vapors/gases
- **c.** volcano/eruption
- **b.** molten/lava
- **d.** destroyed/preserved

10. What does *predict* probably mean?
- **a.** to tell about something before it happens
- **b.** to cause an eruption
- **c.** to warn people
- **d.** to destroy

THINK ABOUT IT

Why do you think authors use different context clues rather than always giving definitions? Write your ideas on a separate sheet of paper.

UNIT 2 REVIEW

Replace each underlined word with a synonym from the box. Write the synonym on the line.

intelligent	humorous	outstanding
peak	tedious	

1. The <u>smart</u> child could read when he was three.

   _____

2. The class play was <u>fabulous</u>. All the students knew their lines. _____

3. The hikers cheered when they reached the <u>summit</u> of the mountain. _____

4. She found the joke <u>amusing</u>, but her friend did not laugh.

   _____

5. The job was so <u>boring</u> that she almost fell asleep.

   _____

Replace each underlined word with an antonym from the box. Write the antonym on the line.

complex	forbid	gigantic
joy	rival	

6. His <u>ally</u> on the other team was a year older than he.

   _____

7. The <u>simple</u> problem took an hour to solve.

   _____

8. The <u>tiny</u> book held a lot of information. _____

9. The principal will <u>allow</u> running in the halls.

_____

10. He cried with <u>sadness</u> when he saw his healthy baby.

_____

Read the following paragraphs. Use context clues to understand the underlined words. Then answer the questions.

Where do penguins live? If you answered "Antarctica," you're right. Many penguins do live there. But did you know that some penguins live in warm climates? One such penguin is the Humboldt penguin. This flightless bird <u>inhabits</u> the coasts of Peru and Chile, countries in South America.

This type of penguin got its name from the Humboldt <u>current</u>, a flow of water in the ocean. The Humboldt penguin depends on the cold water of the current for food. When the water warms up, the food that fish eat disappears, and the fish leave in search of other food. The <u>exodus</u> of fish leads to starvation among the penguins, whose main source of food is fish.

Although weather and other natural events affect the penguins, human action is the greatest threat to their survival. The Humboldt lays its eggs in nests of <u>guano</u>, or bird droppings. Since guano makes good fertilizer, people <u>harvest</u>, or collect, it. This destroys the nests. Humans also fish the waters where the penguins get food, lessening the fish available to the penguins. Sometimes the penguins get caught in fishing nets, too.

11. Which word is a synonym for *lives*?

    a. inhabits   **b.** exodus   **c.** current

12. What is the definition given for the word *current*?

    a. happening now   **b.** a flow of water   **c.** a danger

13. What does the word *exodus* mean?

    a. piles of bird droppings

    b. a flow of cold water

    c. the leaving of a large group

14. Which word means "bird droppings"?

    a. guano   **b.** exodus   **c.** current

15. What does *harvest* mean?

    a. destroy   **b.** collect   **c.** threat

UNIT 2 APPLICATION ACTIVITY
Who Are You?

Think of five words to describe yourself. Write them on the lines below under "Description." Then, write a synonym for each word. Does the list of synonyms still describe you?

      Description   **Synonyms**

_____   _____

_____   _____

_____   _____

_____   _____

_____   _____

UNIT 3

Dictionary Skills

LESSON 7: Finding Words in a Dictionary

GOAL: To learn to use a dictionary to find the meanings of new words

WORDS TO KNOW

alphabetical order   dictionary   entry   guide words

Alphabetical Order

If you cannot figure out a word by breaking it into smaller parts or by looking at the context, you can turn to a dictionary.

A dictionary is a useful tool. It serves many purposes. It shows you how to pronounce words. It provides the correct spelling of words. It tells how words developed. For most people, the main purpose of a dictionary is to give the meaning, or definition, of words.

The words in a dictionary appear in alphabetical order. In a dictionary, you will see words beginning with all the letters of the alphabet. Words beginning with the letter *a* will be at the front of the book. Words starting with the letter *z* will be at the end of the book.

When words begin with the same letter, the second letter decides alphabetical order. For example, *glove* would appear before *gold*. Both words begin with *g*, but *l* comes before *o*.

TIP

Besides definitions, a dictionary tells you how to pronounce words. There will be some kind of key in the dictionary to tell you what the symbols mean. This is especially helpful for long words.

■ PRACTICE 27: Alphabetical Order

Look at the list of words below. Write the words in alphabetical order on the lines.

rehearse	successfully	demonstrate	vehicle
exemplary	ignores	space	evidence
necessity	prescription		

1. _____

2. _____

3. _____

4. _____

5. _____

6. _____

7. _____

8. _____

9. _____

10. _____

Looking for an Entry

Each word defined in a dictionary is called an entry. To find an entry, you use the guide words at the top of each page of the dictionary. The two guide words on each page are the first and last entries on that page. For example, imagine that you want to find the meaning of the word *demonstrate.* Since the letter *d* is near the beginning of the alphabet, you open to the front part of the dictionary. Then you look at the guide words at the top of each page. Look at the following pair of guide words:

democracy • demystify

The word *demonstrate* would come between these two words in alphabetical order. You have found the page on which the word *demonstrate* appears.

What if you wanted to find the word *demonstrating* or *demonstrated?* The various forms of the same verb (action word) appear in the entry with the base word. In this case, the base word is *demonstrate.*

The same is true for words with suffixes. If you do not find an entry for the word you want, look at the entry for the base word. For example, the word *successfully* may not have its own entry. In most dictionaries, this word appears at the end of the entry for the base word, *success.*

TIP

It is a good idea to keep a vocabulary journal. When you come across a new word, write it in your journal. Then write the sentence in which it was used. If you think you know the meaning of the word, write that, too. Later, use a dictionary to check your definition.

■ PRACTICE 28: Looking for an Entry

Look at each word. Then look at the pairs of guide words. Decide which pair of guide words would appear on the same page as the entry given. Circle the letter of your answer.

1. rehearse
   a. religion • republic
   b. redo • refuse
   c. regard • reinvent

2. evidence
   a. every • evil
   b. event • evict
   c. evident • exact

3. vehicle

    a. velvet • verdict

    b. vampire • veil

    c. vain • valance

4. space

    a. squat • state

    b. salmon • scarce

    c. soy • Spanish

5. monolith

    a. monogram • monotony

    b. monotreme • monstrous

    c. monkey • monogerm

6. revile

    a. revere • review

    b. reviewer • revolve

    c. rhetorical • rhizoid

IN REAL LIFE

Besides looking for a word in the dictionary, in what other situations do you use alphabetical order? Write a list below.

_____

_____

_____

_____

LESSON 8: Understanding Definitions

 GOAL: To learn to read dictionary entries to understand and choose definitions

Understanding Definitions

Most people who turn to a dictionary are looking for a definition, or the meaning of a word. A word can have several different meanings. Some meanings appear as simple synonyms. Other meanings need more explanation. Sometimes a helpful example is given. Sometimes a word has more than one entry.

To decide which definition is the one you want, use the context of the sentence. Ask yourself *Which definition makes sense in this sentence?* Look at this sentence:

The spies <u>plotted</u> to steal the secrets.

What does *plotted* mean in this sentence? Read these entries:

¹**plot** *n* **1** a small area of ground. **2** a piece of land in a cemetery. **3** the main story (in a novel or movie). **4** a secret plan.

²**plot** *vb* **1** to mark on a map (plot your route for a trip). **2** to locate by using coordinates (to plot a point in geometry). **3** to plan secretly. **4** to create the plot (of a book or movie).

Which definition is correct for the sentence? It is the second entry (a verb), definition 3.

■ PRACTICE 29: Understanding Definitions

Look at the definitions for *demonstrate* below. Use them to answer the questions that follow. Circle the letter of the correct answer to each question.

> **demonstrate** *vb* **1** to show clearly; reveal. **2** to show or prove by reasoning or evidence: Drug companies must *demonstrate* that their medicines are safe. **3** to show how a product works. **4** to make a public display of opinion.

1. What is a synonym for *demonstrate*?

   a. reveal   **b.** evidence   **c.** make

2. Which of the definitions provides an example sentence?

   a. 1   **b.** 2   **c.** 3

3. Which definition might have used the following example sentence?

   We will carry signs when we *demonstrate* in front of city hall.

   a. 2   **b.** 3   **c.** 4

UNIT 3 REVIEW

Write the words below in alphabetical order.

ambidextrous	ambivalent	alignment
androgen	amorphous	

1. _____

2. _____

3. _____

4. _____

5. _____

Read the vocabulary word. Then read the pairs of guide words. Circle the letter of the guide words that would appear on the same page as the vocabulary word.

6. froufrou
   a. fucold • fume
   b. frighten • frond
   c. froth • fuschia

7. recuse
   a. recrudescence • redact
   b. recompense • recreation
   c. reason • recamier

Read the definitions below. Then use them to answer the questions.

¹**scale** *n* an instrument for weighing.

²**scale** *n* **1** a small, flat plate that forms part of the covering of a fish's body. **2** a thin coating or layer.

³**scale** *vb* **1** to scrape the scales from: He scaled the fish he had caught before frying it. **2** to take off something in thin layers. **3** to throw (a flat stone) so that it skims the water.

⁴scale *vb* **1** to climb up by using a ladder. **2** to reach the highest point: She was the first woman to scale that mountain.

⁵scale *n* a series of musical tones.

8. Which meaning of *scale* makes sense in this sentence? Circle the letter of your answer.

   She found playing scales boring, but her piano teacher made her do it every day.

   a. entry 1   **b.** entry 2, definition 2   **c.** entry 5

9. Write a sample sentence for definition 1.

   _____

   _____

10. Which definition of *scale* makes sense in this sentence? Circle the letter of your answer.

    The knights began to scale the wall, but their foes poured hot oil on their heads.

    a. entry 3, definition 1
    b. entry 4, definition 1
    c. entry 3, definition 3

UNIT 3 APPLICATION ACTIVITY
Using the Dictionary for School

Read ahead in one of your textbooks. Find three words that you do not know. On a separate sheet of paper, write each word and the sentence in which it appears. Look up the words in a dictionary, and write the definitions. If there is more than one definition, use the context to choose the correct one.

UNIT 4

Understanding What You Read

LESSON 9: Identifying Main Ideas

GOAL: To identify the main idea of a paragraph

WORDS TO KNOW

detail	paragraph	topic sentence
main idea	summarizing	

Recognizing a Topic Sentence

Writers divide their stories and articles into paragraphs for a reason. In each paragraph, they discuss one idea. A paragraph is a group of sentences that discusses a single idea—the main idea of the paragraph.

Sometimes this main idea of a paragraph is stated directly. When this is the case, the sentence in which the main idea is stated is the topic sentence. The topic sentence often appears at the very beginning or the very end of the paragraph. (But not always. A topic sentence may appear anywhere in a paragraph.) The topic sentence summarizes all the information in the paragraph. Other sentences provide details. Details are small pieces of information that together support the main idea.

Read this paragraph. Try to find the topic sentence.

Pets can be good for people. They can give people something to care for outside themselves. This can get their minds off problems and help with depression. Some pets give emotional support. Dogs, for example, seem to sense the feelings of their owners. Pets have been shown to lower blood pressure in nursing home patients. Just petting a cat or other soft animal has this effect. Some animals can assist disabled people. Seeing-eye dogs are one example. There are also monkeys and miniature ponies that are trained to help people with daily activities.

Did you find the topic sentence? It is the sentence that sums up what the other sentences are talking about. It is the sentence that is supported by the other sentences. In this paragraph, the topic sentence is also the first sentence: *Pets can be good for people.*

■ PRACTICE 30: Recognizing a Topic Sentence

Read the following paragraph. Then answer the questions that follow. Write your answers on the lines.

(1) In the mid-1660s, two major disasters struck London. (2) In 1665, more than 70,000 Londoners died from a disease called the plague. (3) There were so many dead and dying that they lay about the streets unattended. (4) One year later, fire destroyed more than three fourths of the city. (5) The Great Fire of London burned for over a week and destroyed more than 30,000 homes.

1. What is the main idea of this paragraph? _____

   _____

2. Which sentence is the topic sentence? (Give the sentence number.) _____

3. Explain your choice for the topic sentence. _____

   _____

4. Why is sentence 5 not a good topic sentence? _____

   _____

Summarizing a Paragraph in a Title

Sometimes a main idea is clearly stated in a topic sentence. Sometimes, however, there is no topic sentence. The main idea is expressed throughout the paragraph.

When there is no topic sentence in a paragraph, there are other ways to find the main idea. One way is by summing up, or summarizing, the topic in a word or phrase. Sometimes these words or phrases can be used as titles. Writing a title that summarizes the paragraph is a good way to find the main idea.

Any title must relate only to what actually appears in the paragraph. It must be narrow, or specific, enough that it only covers what is in the paragraph. It must also be broad enough to cover *all* of the paragraph's information.

Read the following paragraph. Then summarize the paragraph by writing a title with the correct focus.

It had been raining heavily several days before the flood. A dam fourteen miles above Johnstown was weakening under the rising rainwater. The dam had not been properly kept up over the years. At mid-afternoon on May 31, 1889, the dam collapsed. A wall of churning water swept down the valley. Houses, trees, trains, animals, telegraph poles, and over 2,200 people were swept away by the forceful rush.

This paragraph tells a story. It does not have a clearly stated topic sentence. You have to ask yourself what the paragraph is about, then try to summarize that idea in a word or phrase.

"Water Can Be Dangerous" does not work. Although the paragraph does tell about a case in which water was dangerous, the paragraph only tells about one situation. You would need more paragraphs to cover the general topic of dangerous water. You would need to include stories of rough seas, of flash floods, of household accidents involving water, and more. This topic is too broad.

"The Loss of Telegraph Poles in the Johnstown Flood" does not work, either. It is too narrow. Telegraph poles are mentioned, but they were just one type of item lost.

"The Collapse of the Dam above Johnstown" is a better title. It lets you know what the paragraph is about. The paragraph tells why the dam collapsed and what happened when it did.

■ PRACTICE 31: Summarizing a Paragraph in a Title

Read the following paragraph. Then answer the question. Circle the letter of the correct answer.

Why are there no forests in the desert? The answer is that trees use and give off a large amount of water every day, especially during hot weather. This process is called *transpiration*. The trees need the water, together with sunlight and carbon dioxide, for photosynthesis, or plant food production. They suck up the water with their roots and release it into the air as water vapor through their leaves. Scientists estimate that the average tree transpires 80 gallons of water a day and as much as 150 gallons during hot weather. A large oak tree will give off 28,000 gallons of water during one growing season!

1. Which is the best title for this paragraph?
   a. "Large Oaks in Hot Weather"
   b. "Desert Forests"
   c. "Thirsty Trees"
   d. "Scientists' Study of Trees and Water"

Read the following paragraph. Then write a title for it.

Early American colonists along the New England coast found an abundance of little grayish berries. The berries were no good as food, but they were not useless. The colonists got a clear tallow, a waxlike substance, from these bayberries. The colonists found that the tallow produced excellent candles. Even in the hot summer, the bayberry candles stayed hard. In the middle of winter, they gave off a pleasant summery scent. Soon bayberry candles were lighting homes throughout the American colonies.

2. Title: _____

THINK ABOUT IT

Newspapers summarize stories in titles all the time. These titles are called *headlines,* and they appear above articles. Why do you think newspapers use headlines? What kinds of headlines catch your attention? Write your answers on a separate sheet of paper.

Identifying the Question

You have learned two ways to pinpoint the main idea of a paragraph. One way is to find a topic sentence that is supported by the other sentences in the paragraph. Another way is to summarize what a paragraph is about in a few words. Identifying the question a paragraph answers is yet another way.

Every paragraph should answer one question. In searching for the main idea of a paragraph, try to phrase the single question that the paragraph, as a whole, answers. Let's try this out. Read the following paragraph:

> (1) Mustangs are wild horses. (2) For hundreds of years, they have freely roamed the plains of the United States. (3) Their natural enemies are wolves and mountain lions. (4) Both attack the horses by first jumping on their backs. (5) Therefore, when a saddle or rider sits on a mustang's back, its first instinct is to buck wildly. (6) Using spurs on the wild horse makes the situation even worse. (7) The spurs feel like the claws of the lion or wolf and make the mustang buck even more wildly.

This paragraph gives a lot of information about mustangs. What specific question about mustangs does it answer? The first four sentences give general information about mustang behavior. Sentence five explains why this background causes the horses to react the way they do to riders. The last two sentences add more information about how the horses react to more contact.

Why are mustangs so difficult to ride? captures what the paragraph is answering. The main idea, then, can be stated as an answer like this: Mustangs are difficult to ride because they react to riding gear as though they are being attacked in the wild.

■ PRACTICE 32: Identifying the Question

Read the following paragraph. Then answer the question. Circle the letter of the correct answer.

> Broken bones can be either compound or simple fractures. These terms do not refer to the number of breaks in the bone. A simple fracture happens when the bone does not pierce the skin after it is broken. A compound fracture is one in which the bone breaks and pierces the skin. Most broken bones are simple fractures, even if the bone is broken in two or more places. If the bone pierces the skin and a bleeding wound forms, however, it is a compound fracture.

Which question does this paragraph answer? Circle the letter of your answer.

a. What are compound fractures?

b. What are simple fractures?

c. What is the difference between compound and simple fractures?

d. How can broken bones cause flesh wounds?

LESSON 10: Drawing Conclusions

GOAL: To learn to draw conclusions from information in a
paragraph

WORDS TO KNOW

cause	conclusion	effect
compare	contrast	generalize

Drawing Conclusions

Most paragraphs do more than just list information and ideas.
They also suggest things. If you think carefully about what you
read, you will learn how to "read between the lines" to draw
conclusions. A conclusion is what you figure out even though it
has not been stated. For example, if a writer advises, "Never go
skiing alone," you can conclude that it must be dangerous to
ski alone.

Drawing conclusions is part art and part science. You must
use your imagination to "read between the lines." But you must
also be able to defend your conclusions with facts and details
from the paragraph. Your conclusion may be true, but if the
paragraph does not support it, your conclusion is not valid,
or acceptable. Read the following paragraph:

> (1) Like people, sick trees get fevers. (2) Scientists
> discovered this while working with forest rangers.
> (3) They used a heat-sensing device as they flew over
> forests in helicopters. (4) Ailing trees gave off more heat
> than healthy trees did. (5) Scientists also discovered that

Unit 4: **Understanding What You Read** • Vocabulary and Reading Comprehension trees' fevers are highest in the morning. (6) People, unlike trees, experience their highest fevers at night.

You can draw more than one conclusion from this paragraph. First, you can conclude that scientists must have conducted heat-sensing tests of sick trees at various times of the day. Otherwise, sentence 5 would not be able to say that "trees' fevers are highest in the morning." A second conclusion is that all trees give off heat. Sentence 4 states "ailing trees gave off more heat than healthy trees." Both conclusions are supported by details in the paragraph.

You might also guess that the scientists worked for the National Park Service. Although this may be true, there is no detail in the paragraph to support this conclusion. Therefore, it is not a valid, or an acceptable, conclusion.

TIP

Do not jump to conclusions! Sometimes we believe something is true, even if there is no evidence to support it. Think your conclusions through to be sure that the reading supports them. This is especially important on tests.

■ PRACTICE 33: Drawing Conclusions

Read the following paragraph. Then answer the questions. Circle the letter of the correct answer to each question.

Did you know that most oysters sold in restaurants are farmed? Oyster farmers plant and harvest, or collect, oysters in bays. First, the farmers clear an area of the bay floor. They firm the bottom with shells and tiles. Then, they mark their oyster crops with surface buoys, or floating markers. Farmers have to deal with the many fish and other sea creatures that feed on oysters. An oyster's chance for reaching adulthood is about one in a million. Those that survive are dredged, or pulled, from the bay floor and sold to seafood markets.

1. The first sentence suggests that
   a. there are very few restaurants that sell oysters.
   b. most people think oysters are fished, not farmed.
   c. most people do not like to eat oysters.
   d. oysters are an endangered species.

2. What can you conclude about oyster farmers?
   a. Oyster farmers own the bay floor they farm.
   b. Oyster farmers do not have many oysters to sell, even though they work hard.
   c. Oyster farmers never need to go in the water.
   d. Oyster farmers fence animals that eat oysters out of their farms.

3. For every adult oyster dredged from the bay, about how many oysters fall prey to fish and other sea creatures that feed on oysters?
   a. a dozen   c. a thousand
   b. a hundred   d. a million

4. You can conclude that oysters grow poorly
   a. in salt water.
   b. on loose sandy bay floors.
   c. on bay floors covered with shells.
   d. in freshwater.

Drawing Conclusions from Details

Some conclusions just make observations about details or restate them in a different way. For instance, if a paragraph states that the police "can identify from its markings which gun fired a bullet," you can conclude that each gun leaves a unique marking just as a person's fingerprint does. Sometimes details in a reading can suggest time or place. The detail "full moon" suggests the action is taking place at night. The detail "Big Ben struck six" suggests the action is taking place in London.

Read the following paragraph:

> Salt has been an important trading item for human beings for thousands of years. One of the oldest Roman roads was named Via Salaria, or Salt Road. It led from Rome to the salt beds of Ostia. There, salt was mined and carried back to Rome. It was valued so much that each soldier in the Roman Army was given a regular allowance of it. In fact, the word *salary* comes from the Roman word for salt. Also, the expression, "Worth one's salt," suggests the value associated with this treasure.

You can conclude from this passage that the Romans used salt as a payment for debts. The fact that the salt was mined from beds indicates that it was close to the earth's surface and not deep in the earth. It is also likely that Ostia was the major source of salt for the Romans. Roman soldiers must also have valued salt, since it was given as an allowance in place of money. If they had no use for it, they would have rebelled.

Drawing conclusions means collecting evidence and thinking about what it means. People do this with texts. They also do it with other people.

Think about how someone's speech, dress, manners, and gestures affect how you view him or her. You draw conclusions from these things. Remember, people draw conclusions about you, too.

■ PRACTICE 34: Drawing Conclusions from Details

Read the following paragraph and see what conclusions you can draw from the details. Then answer the questions that follow. Circle the letter of the answer that completes the sentence.

"Survival of the fittest" does not mean an animal must be quick and intelligent. A sloth is slow-moving and not very intelligent. One might think that sloths are easily caught and eaten by predators. However, the opposite is true. Sloths spend most of their time hanging upside down in trees. Since they move so slowly, many animals that would eat them do not even notice them. They survive because of their slowness! In fact, their species has managed to survive for millions of years.

1. You can conclude that species that _____ will survive.

    a. are intelligent   **c.** can avoid being eaten

    b. are fast-moving   **d.** are slow and stupid

2. You can conclude that many predators depend on
_____ for locating food.
   a. their eyesight
   b. movement of the food animals
   c. their sense of smell
   d. their sense of balance

3. If sloths moved faster, they might be _____.
   a. more plentiful   **c.** right side up in trees
   b. extinct   **d.** a more successful species

Generalizing

Generalizing is a way of drawing a conclusion. You generalize when you make a broad statement based on specific details. Read this paragraph:

> The Polynesians had no compass, but they used stars, waves, currents, clouds, and birds to guide them. They knew how each star changed position throughout the year.

This paragraph gives details about how the Polynesians used the natural world. You can conclude from these details that Polynesians observed their world closely. This is a generalization about them. It is a broad statement based on the individual details.

Try generalizing about the details in the following paragraph:

> Some birds control the area, or territory, around their nests. Birds protect their families from intruders. They do not want predators to eat their young. So they try to scare

off animals. And they do not want other birds to take up important resources. These resources include food and nesting material. The size of the territory depends on the amount of materials available and the needs of the bird.

From this information, you can generalize that having a set territory helps birds get what they need for themselves and their young.

■ PRACTICE 35: Generalizing

Read the following paragraphs. Then answer the questions that follow. Circle the letter of the correct answer.

In every hive, there is a crew of bees that keeps things clean. They make sure that the wax cells that will hold honey are free of dirt. If a bee dies in the hive, they carry it far away. If a larger animal gets in the hive and dies, they mummify it in a bee glue. This way, they prevent the spread of disease.

1. Which generalization about bees is supported by the paragraph?
   a. Bees have a complex burial ritual.
   b. Bees are concerned about staying healthy.
   c. Bees instinctively kill any animal that gets into their hive.
   d. Bees preserve the bodies of the dead members in the same way as the ancient Egyptians.

2. This paragraph shows that bees are very

    a. territorial.   **c.** organized.

    b. aggressive.   **d.** stupid.

Tagging is a practice used by scientists to keep track of animals in the wild. Tagging helps scientists determine the movement and habits of the animals under study. Scientists have studied lobsters in this way. When tagged lobsters are caught again, they are often found close to where they were set free. Most have moved less than a mile. The longest distance a tagged lobster traveled was 60 miles.

3. Which generalization about tagging studies is supported by the paragraph?

    a. Scientists tag animals because they cannot tell the difference between individual animals.

    b. Tagging studies take place mainly in the sea.

    c. All scientists perform tagging experiments.

    d. Tagging studies increase our knowledge of how animals behave.

4. Which generalization about lobsters is supported by this paragraph?

    a. Lobsters do not move or migrate very much.

    b. Lobsters are very slow-moving creatures.

    c. Tagging lobsters causes them to slow down.

    d. Lobsters cannot swim very well.

Recognizing Compare-and-Contrast Words

Sometimes you can use the information in a paragraph to compare and contrast. When you compare one thing to another, you show how they are alike. When you contrast things, you show how they are different.

Here are some words that signal comparison and contrast:

Compare Words	Contrast Words
like	differ
likewise	different
same	however
similar	in contrast
similarly	on the other hand
too	unlike

Read these sentences:

Callie walked to school when the weather was clear. Like Callie, Kerry liked to get exercise on the way to school. Gabbi, on the other hand, chose to ride the bus.

Which girls are being compared? Callie and Kerry. The signal word *like* tells you that Callie and Kerry have something in common. They are the same in some way.

Gabbi is being contrasted with the other girls. She does something different. The contrast signal words are *on the other hand.*

■ PRACTICE 36: Recognizing Compare-and-Contrast Words

Read the sentences below. Decide whether things are being compared or contrasted. Write *compare* or *contrast* on the line provided.

1. Grant loves sports. Conor is a sports fan, too. _____

2. Grant's favorite sport is football. Conor, on the other hand, prefers soccer. _____

3. Unlike his brothers, Ricky prefers music. _____

4. The boys' taste in music differs. Ricky likes hip-hop, but Darby is into jazz. _____

Comparing and Contrasting

You can gain new knowledge by comparing and contrasting. You can also look at things in a new way. Comparing and contrasting helps you draw conclusions about things in relation to each other.

Read the following paragraph:

> No one knows for sure how many people lived in what is now the United States in 1492, when Columbus voyaged to the New World. Some experts estimate that there were over a million Native Americans at that time. By 1900, that figure had fallen to less than half a million. Since the 1950s, however, the Native American population has grown rapidly. Today, more than two million Native Americans live in the United States.

In comparing present and past Native American populations, you can draw several conclusions. You can conclude that the Native American population dropped severely between 1492 and 1900. The present Native American population is twice that of the fifteenth century. The word *however* points out a change in the pattern of the past.

You can also conclude that the Native American population will likely be larger in the future, since that has been the trend for over 50 years. This means the trends that caused the dropping population have not been present over the past 50 years. You might be correct in guessing that the arrival of the European explorers and white settlers led to the drop. But there are no facts in the paragraph to support this conclusion.

■ PRACTICE 37: Comparing and Contrasting

Read the following paragraph. Then circle the letter of the correct answer to each question.

Long before coal fueled Europe's industrial revolution in the 1700s, the Chinese were using it to heat their homes. In contrast to the vast forests of Europe, the treeless plains of northern China provided no wood for fuel. But there were large deposits of coal close to the surface. Chinese peasants found that coal caught fire and burned slowly. So they regularly used it as a fuel more than a thousand years before it was used in Europe.

1. Which comparison is supported by the paragraph?
   a. The Chinese are more clever than the Europeans.
   b. The Chinese had a greater need than the Europeans to find a fuel source like coal.
   c. The Chinese have more coal deposits than the Europeans do.
   d. China's coal is easier to mine than Europe's.

2. Europeans may have discovered and used coal sooner if
   a. their fuel needs had not been met by trees.
   b. they had been as intelligent as the Chinese.
   c. they had needed a slow-burning fuel.
   d. they had explored China sooner.

3. From this paragraph, you can conclude that
   a. there is more coal in China than in Europe.
   b. Chinese peasants preferred coal to wood.
   c. coal has long been used as an energy source.
   d. Europe's climate is warmer than China's.

THINK ABOUT IT

You may remember Venn diagrams from math class. A Venn diagram is made up of two (or three) circles that overlap. In math, you use a Venn diagram to group sets of things. You can also use a Venn diagram to compare and contrast things. Just label the two circles with what you are comparing and contrasting. Where the circles overlap, write what the two things have in common—this is where you compare them. In the part of each circle that is not overlapping, write what is true for that thing. This graphic organizer can help you compare and contrast ideas in a visual way.

Recognizing Cause-and-Effect Relationships

Often the information in a paragraph shows a link between cause and effect. A cause results in something happening. An effect is what happens.

Here are some words that signal cause and effect:

because	consequently	leads to	results in
since	so	therefore	

Look at these examples:

Because I got a flat tire, I was late for the show.

I went alone, since Ann did not want to go.

In the first sentence, the cause is a flat tire, and the effect is that I was late. *Because* is a word that signals a cause-and-effect relationship.

In the second sentence, what is the cause? Ann did not want to go. What is the effect? I went alone. Do you see the signal word? It is *since.*

■ PRACTICE 38: Recognizing Cause-and-Effect Relationships

Underline each cause once. Underline each effect twice.

1. Samantha took Smoky to the vet because he had a cut on his nose.
2. The doctor was busy, so Samantha had to wait.
3. Because he was in pain, the dog whimpered.
4. The dog needed stitches because the wound was deep.
5. Smoky was healthy and young; therefore, his cut healed quickly.

Outcome of Cause-and-Effect Relationships

Recognizing cause-and-effect relationships helps you predict an outcome. This means you conclude what is likely to happen, based on information you have read.

Look for cause-and-effect relationships in the following paragraph:

> Technology has improved the ability of disabled persons to get around. Now there is a high-tech wheelchair that can follow its owner's spoken orders. A completely paralyzed person can operate it, because it responds to voice commands. The chair has a computer that can recognize 32 voice commands. Since accidents and confusion are potential problems, this wheelchair has been designed to recognize only the voice of its owner.

New technology causes some things to happen. It has led to a new wheelchair. What are some effects of this technology? One effect is that more people who are completely paralyzed will be able to go places. You can also conclude that if a friend of the owner tried to operate the wheelchair, it would not move. "Only the voice of its owner" will make the wheelchair go. Based on this paragraph, you can predict that as computer technology improves, wheelchairs will become even more user-friendly.

THINK ABOUT IT

A flow chart is a kind of cause-and-effect chart. It tells what happens if something else happens. A flow chart can be just a series of boxes with an arrow between boxes showing which way the action is going. Creating a chart like this when you read can help you see causes and effects more clearly.

■ PRACTICE 39: Outcome of Cause-and-Effect Relationships

Read the following paragraph. Then circle the letter of the correct answer to each question.

> We do not need fancy equipment to predict the weather. Satellite photographs are unnecessary. We merely need to tune in to nature. Trees, animals, and clouds all respond to changes in air pressure. Crickets chirp faster if the temperature rises. Birds do not fly as much when a storm is approaching. Instead, they tend to remain perched in trees. If there is morning dew on the grass, the chances for fair weather are good. Nature is filled with hundreds of little clues we can use to predict weather changes.

1. What will the effect be if there is an approaching storm?
   a. Crickets will chirp more slowly.
   b. Birds will remain perched in trees.
   c. There will be no morning dew on the grass.
   d. all of the above

2. Which cause-and-effect relationship is supported by the paragraph?
   a. Weather satellites first enabled us to predict the weather.
   b. Animals can cause weather changes.
   c. Changes in air pressure affect the weather.
   d. Changes in air pressure keep birds from flying.

LESSON 11: Recognizing Sequence

GOAL: To improve reading comprehension by recognizing sequence

WORDS TO KNOW

future tense	past tense	sequence
past perfect tense	present tense	verb tenses

Identifying Verb Tenses

Sequence refers to the order in which things happen. Every story has a series of events. The order in which the events happen is the sequence.

Understanding sequence is important to understanding and remembering what you read. Imagine that you are studying the American Civil War. Was the Emancipation Proclamation, the document ending slavery, signed before or after the start of the war? The order of events can make a big difference to understanding why things happen.

Writers give clues about when things happen. One way to tell about order is to use correct verb tenses. Verb tenses are forms of verbs (action words) that tell when things happen in relation to one another. Verb tenses include the past, present, and future:

past tense: shows that something happened before now

present tense: shows that something is happening now, or it happens regularly (as a habit or routine)

future tense: shows that something will happen later

Look at the following sentences:

> past tense: Flora bought her bread at the corner store. (She may have done this earlier today, or last week, or any time in the past.)

> present tense: Flora buys her bread at the corner store. (Flora is doing this now, or she does it regularly.)

> future tense: Flora will buy her bread at the corner store. (Flora will do this later today, or next week, or sometime in the future.)

These simple tenses are easy to follow. The past perfect tense, however, can be confusing. Writers use the past perfect tense when they want to show that a past action came before another past action. Look at this example:

> past perfect tense: Flora had bought her bread before she went to work.

■ PRACTICE 40: Identifying Verb Tenses

Read the following sentences. Tell whether each sentence is in the past, present, future, or past perfect tense. Write your answer on the line.

1. Derek shops at the new mall. _____

2. Derek got a new jacket. _____

3. It will be cold soon. _____

4. Derek chose a wool jacket, but his mother had bought him a nylon one already. _____

PRACTICE 41: Using Verb Tenses to Recognize Sequence

Read the following passage. Pay attention to the verb tenses. Then put the events in the correct order. Number them 1 through 5, with 1 being the first event.

The telephone startled Lisa. She had dozed off in front of the television after supper. Still half asleep, she answered the phone. An official-sounding voice asked, "Is this Ms. LaSalle?"

Shakily, Lisa said, "Yes, it is."

"This is Sergeant Jantzen at the police station. Do you have a son Darren?"

Lisa tried to steady her voice. Again, she answered, "Yes." What could be wrong?

"Your son has been injured in an accident. He was not wearing his seat belt. He's at City General."

"Thank-you. I'll be right there," Lisa answered. Just that morning, Lisa had reminded Darren about the seat belt!

_____ The telephone woke Lisa.

_____ Lisa talked to Darren about wearing a seat belt.

_____ Lisa had supper.

_____ Lisa fell asleep.

_____ Sergeant Jantzen told Lisa about the accident.

Identifying Time Clues

Writers use verb tenses to place events in time. They also use time words. These time words give clues about when things happen in relation to other things.

Here are some time words that tell you that two things are happening at the same time:

at the same time	during	meanwhile
simultaneously	when	while

Here are some words that tell you when things happen in relation to one another:

before	after	first
second	third	next
then	last	finally

Here are some words that place events in a time frame:

now	today	yesterday
tomorrow	the next day	the day after
the day before	next week	last year

■ PRACTICE 42: Identifying Time Clues

Underline the time clues in the following paragraph.

Today is my birthday! First, I am going to have breakfast with my grandparents. Then I plan to go to the mall with my best friend. When we have finished shopping, we will go back to my house. Maybe we'll watch a video after lunch. Later I'll try on my new clothes and show my mom. I think my friends have something planned for tonight!

PRACTICE 43: Using Time Clues to Recognize Sequence

Read the paragraph. Pay attention to the time clues. Then put the events in the correct order. Number them 1 through 9, with 1 being the first event.

When Maggie was five, her grandfather took her on an airplane ride. He had learned to fly in the Air Force during the Vietnam War. After the war, he had been hired as an airline pilot. Later, he had bought his own small airplane. Although Maggie was frightened at takeoff, she was thrilled when the plane leveled off. After that first flight, she nagged her granddad to teach her to fly. At age eight, she was allowed to take control of the plane while it was in the air. At age ten, she learned to take off and land. Before each lesson, she and her father would review everything she had learned. By the time Maggie entered high school, she was an accomplished flyer.

_____ Maggie became an accomplished flyer.

_____ Maggie's grandfather was hired as an airline pilot.

_____ Maggie learned to take off and land.

_____ Maggie's grandfather bought his own plane.

_____ Maggie was allowed to take control of the plane in the air.

_____ Maggie took her first airplane ride.

_____ Maggie's grandfather joined the Air Force.

_____ Maggie nagged her grandfather to teach her to fly.

_____ Maggie's grandfather learned to fly.

Specific Times

Besides giving clues to help you place events in order, authors use specific times. They tell you during which year, in what season, during which month, and at what time of day events happened. Or they may refer to decades, centuries, or other spans of time.

Here are some examples of specific time words:

Friday	in the morning	at 10:05 A.M.
last fall	March	1985
the 1800s	while Henry VIII ruled	

■ PRACTICE 44: Specific Times

Read the paragraph. Then answer the questions about time. Circle the letter of the answer to each question.

At 11:30, Jake came home from soccer practice. The summer league season had just started, and Jake wasn't used to all the running yet. He found a note from his mother on the table. It reminded him that today was Thursday. Jake had a piano lesson every Thursday afternoon at 3:00. Mr. Howells, the piano teacher, lived just across the street. Jake decided he had time to shower, eat lunch, and take a nap before his lesson. He headed for the shower.

1. In what season does this story take place?

   a. spring

   c. fall

   b. summer

   d. winter

2. During what part of the day did Jake get home from soccer practice?

    a. morning   **c.** evening

    b. afternoon   **d.** night

3. During what part of the day was Jake's piano lesson?

    a. morning   **c.** evening

    b. afternoon   **d.** night

4. Which of these events happened first?

    a. Jake went to soccer practice.

    b. Jake read the note.

    c. Jake headed for the shower.

    d. Jake came home from practice.

5. Which of these events happened last?

    a. Jake went to soccer practice.

    b. Jake read the note.

    c. Jake headed for the shower.

    d. Jake came home from practice.

UNIT 4 REVIEW

Read the paragraphs. Then answer the questions.

(1) With its world-famous resources, New York has a healthy tourism industry. (2) Visitors from around the globe enter the United States through New York City. (3) They marvel at the skyscrapers, bridges, museums, and shopping districts, and the hectic pace of this busy

city. (4) The Statue of Liberty in New York Harbor has become a symbol of the nation. (5) The Metropolitan Museum of Art contains one of the world's leading collections. (6) Niagara Falls, near Buffalo, is a scenic wonder. (7) Tourists can also escape to nature in the magical Hudson River Valley, the Catskills, the Finger Lakes, the Adirondacks, and the beaches of Long Island.

1. What is the main idea of this paragraph? _____

_____

2. In which sentence is the main idea stated? _____

(1) New York's vast sources of water power much of the state's electricity needs. (2) Its soil and climate make it a leading agricultural state. It produces much of the nation's milk, grapes, and apples. Forests cover about half the state. In its mountain ranges are large deposits of iron ore and zinc.

3. Write a title that sums up the main idea of this paragraph.

_____

Miniature ponies are being trained to be guide animals. Like guide dogs, the ponies help their owners move around in the world. Unlike dogs, ponies do not have a strong need for affection. They are not easily distracted by petting and grooming. Noisy situations do not bother them, either. Horses have served throughout history in wars and have been known to lead their riders to safety through raging battles. Miniature ponies also have a long life span. They generally live to between 30 and 40 years old. This means that their human partners are less likely to have to deal with the grief of losing a trusted guide animal. Guide horses have excellent vision even in low light. With their eyes on the sides of their heads, they can spot danger from almost any direction. Guide horses can be a good choice for people who are allergic to or afraid of service dogs.

4. What question does this paragraph answer? Write the question here. This should be the main idea of the paragraph._____

_____

5. What two things are being compared in this paragraph?

_____

6. Which generalization can you make from this paragraph? Circle the letter of your answer.
   a. Horses can make good guide animals.
   b. Horses are better guide animals than dogs.
   c. Horses are less expensive than guide dogs.

7. Which conclusion can you draw from this paragraph?
   a. Horses are better service animals than dogs because they have better eyesight.
   b. Dogs are usually better service animals than horses.
   c. There are reasons that make a horse a better choice than a dog for some people.

8. Which of the following is an example of a cause-and-effect relationship?

a. Like guide dogs, miniature ponies help their owners move around in the world.

b. Horses have served throughout history in wars and have been known to lead their riders to safety through raging battles.

c. With their eyes on the sides of their heads, they can spot danger from almost any direction.

The Boston Tea Party was one event that led to the American Revolutionary War. England controlled the tea that came into the colonies. In 1767, England had put new taxes on many products, including tea. These taxes were known as the Townsend Acts. After the colonists boycotted, or refused to buy, British products, England removed the taxes—except for the one on tea. In May 1773, England passed the Tea Act. This allowed the British East India Company to sell tea directly to people without going through merchants, or people who made their living selling tea. In December of that year, a group calling themselves the Sons of Liberty dressed up as American Indians and dumped tons of tea from British ships into Boston Harbor. In response to this action, known as the Boston Tea Party, the English government passed four laws, known together as the Intolerable Acts. These laws gave England more power over the colonies. Rather than making it easier for England to control the colonies, however, the Intolerable Acts led the colonies to band together. In 1774, the colonies held the First Continental Congress.

9. Put the following events in the correct sequence. Number them from 1 to 5, with 1 being first.

_____ England passed the Townsend Acts.

_____ England passed the Intolerable Acts.

_____ The Boston Tea Party took place.

_____ The colonies held the First Continental Congress.

_____ England passed the Tea Act.

10. Which conclusion is valid, based on the paragraph?

    a. The Sons of Liberty were great men.

    b. England was too far away to control the colonies.

    c. Taxes were an important issue for the colonies.

UNIT 4 APPLICATION ACTIVITY
It's All in the Sequence

Think about an activity that you enjoy. Write a paragraph that explains how to do that activity. Remember to use sequence words such as first, then, next, finally, before, after, and so on. Write the steps in your activity on the lines on the next page.

_____

_____

_____

_____

_____

_____

_____

Now go back and circle all the sequence words. Read the steps without these words. Are the directions still easy to follow? Or are they less clear? On the lines below, explain how sequence words help make directions clear.

_____

_____

_____

_____

_____

_____

_____

_____

_____

UNIT 5

Finding Information in a Passage

LESSON 12: Scanning

 GOAL: To find information quickly in reading passages by scanning

WORDS TO KNOW

bold type	headlines	scanning
graphics	key words	visual aids
headings	scan	

Scanning for Key Words

One purpose for reading is to find information. Perhaps you are looking for an answer to a question in a textbook. Maybe you want to find the date and time of an event in a newspaper article. If you develop the ability to scan, you can find information more quickly and easily.

Scanning does not mean reading closely. When you scan, you do not read every word. Scanning means looking at a passage and focusing on important elements.

One thing to look for is key words. Key words are words that relate to what you want to find out.

Imagine that you are reading an article about ancient Egypt. What you are really interested in is the mummies found in the pyramids. The reigns of different pharaohs and Egyptian history are not what you want to know about right now. What key words would you scan for? You would probably have good luck with *mummy* and *pyramids.*

Follow these steps when you scan a passage for key words:

1. Decide what you are looking for.

2. Choose key words that relate to what you are looking for.

3. Quickly look over the passage for a key word.

4. When you find a key word, slow down and read that sentence or section. Does it contain the information you want? If so, read the section carefully.

5. If not, continue scanning.

6. If you do not find your key word, choose a new one and scan again.

TIP

When you review for a test, you probably look at the review questions first. Then you look for the answers in the textbook. This is a good plan when you are taking a test involving a reading passage, too.

If it is allowed, read the questions before reading the passage. That way, you'll know what you are looking for. This is useful because it saves time. That can be important on a timed test.

■ PRACTICE 45: Scanning for Key Words

Carefully read each question on the next page. Write one or two key words from the question on the first line provided. Then scan the article titled "An Exceptional Land" to find the answers. After scanning, write the answer to each question.

1. What kind of shellfish is caught off the coast of California?

   Key Words: _____

   Answer: _____

2. What part of California leads the nation in aircraft manufacturing?

   Key Words: _____

   Answer: _____

3. Where are most of California's largest cities located?

   Key Words: _____

   Answer: _____

4. Where is the lowest point in California?

   Key Words: _____

   Answer: _____

5. What are some unusual agricultural products grown in California?

   Key Words: _____

   Answer: _____

An Exceptional Land

Where in the United States can you go snow skiing in the morning and then water skiing in the afternoon? The answer is California. This third-largest state in the Union is a land of extremes. Mt. Whitney, the highest peak of the continental United States, is there. Barely 100 miles away is Death Valley, the lowest point in the country. Rich farmlands are only miles from blazing deserts, which are next door to frigid mountain peaks.

One fourth of Californians are employed in manufacturing in and around Los Angeles and San Francisco. They build defense and transportation equipment, such as cars, ships, boats, and airplanes. In fact, southern California is the nation's largest center for aircraft manufacturing. Silicon Valley, located near San Francisco, is famous for computer technology. Another important industry is the canning and freezing of farm produce.

California leads the states in farming. It accounts for 90 percent of the grapes grown in the United States. It leads the nation in providing lettuce, celery, tomatoes, peaches, and peas. Some of its uncommon farm products— avocados, artichokes, olives, dates, figs, and almonds— are suited only to California's unique climate and growing season. The state rivals Florida and Texas in the production of citrus fruits.

California is second only to Alaska in commercial fishing. Most of the yearly catch of 850 million pounds comes through the ports of San Pedro and San Diego. Tuna, salmon, flounder, mackerel, and sardines are important fishing catches. Shellfish, such as crabs, clams, and lobsters, are also found along the coast.

California has several of the largest cities in the United States. The largest California city, and the second-largest in the nation, is Los Angeles. It is one of the fastest-growing cities in the United States. It has a diverse economy supported by the food production, aircraft, and movie industries. It has some of the most heavily traveled freeways in the world. San Diego is the second-largest city in California, followed by San José. San Francisco ranks fourth. Most of California's large cities are on the coast. Of the top ten, only Sacramento and Fresno are inland.

Other Text Elements

Sometimes, key words or information is called out for you. For example, in textbooks, headings often divide the text into sections. There are usually headlines at the top of a newspaper article. A heading or headline may point out exactly where you can find your information.

In textbooks, you may see words in bold type. These are often key words—they may be the ones you are looking for.

■ PRACTICE 46: Other Text Elements

Read the following questions. Then scan for the answers in "City of Gold." After you have read the passage, write your answers.

1. Explorers from what country settled San Francisco?

   _____

2. Who discovered gold in San Francisco? _____

3. What happened in San Francisco in 1989?

_____

4. What two famous bridges are found in San Francisco?

_____

City of Gold

Early Settlement

San Francisco was originally settled by the **Spanish** because of its fine natural **harbor.** But besides a Spanish mission and port facilities, the city did not grow very fast. By 1845, its population was only 200. Although the city had a rugged beauty, it was always foggy and cold. Many people found it very difficult to build on the **extremely steep hills.** Some pioneers preferred the milder climate farther south. Others farmed the rich land in what is now California's Central Valley.

Striking Gold

In 1848, something amazing happened. A man named **James Marshall** saw something glittering in the stream at the site of a sawmill being built for John Sutter. A closer inspection proved that the stream was flowing with **gold!** When news of gold in San Francisco reached eastern cities and Europe, the **gold rush** was on. By **1849,** the population increased from under 1,000 to over 25,000. Adventurers from the eastern cities and Europe joined wagon trains and moved westward to stake their claims. Since gold attracted gold diggers, gamblers, and gunmen, San Francisco became a wild town.

Earthquakes

San Francisco has long outlived its shady past. It has also survived more than its share of catastrophes. In **1906,** a major earthquake hit the city. Hundreds of buildings collapsed. In the aftermath, much of the city was destroyed by fire. More recently, in **1989,** a major earthquake struck the area, destroying bridge spans and claiming many lives. San Franciscans must prepare for another "big one" to strike at any time.

Features—Natural and Human-Made

San Francisco is built on **42 hills** and overlooks the **largest natural harbor** on America's West Coast. It is a city of gleaming white towers of glass and steel. Whether sunny or foggy, its beauty and charm are breathtaking. Many of San Francisco's hills are famous. Many of the first great mining and railroad men of the city built mansions on Nob Hill. A large colony of Italian-Americans settled on Telegraph Hill. Russian Hill is named after Russian sailors who died during an expedition in the early 1800s and were buried there. Two famous bridges cross San Francisco Bay. The **Golden Gate Bridge,** which is actually red, has one of the longest bridge spans in the world at

4,200 feet. The **San Francisco Bay Bridge** to Oakland is one of the longest bridges in the world.

Scanning for Topic Sentences

If you do not find key words or heads in a passage, try scanning for topic sentences in the paragraphs. Read the first few lines and the last few lines of each paragraph. Often, a topic sentence appears at the beginning or end of a paragraph. If you find the topic sentence, you will get the main idea—and you may find the information you want.

■ PRACTICE 47: Scanning for Topic Sentences

The following article, "The Island Nation," did not appear in a textbook. It has no heads or bold words to point you toward information.

Read the following questions. After scanning the article for topic sentences, answer the questions.

1. Where is Northern Ireland in relation to the main island of the United Kingdom? _____

2. When did the British begin building their empire?

   _____

3. Why did Great Britain start colonies throughout the world?

   _____

The Island Nation

A short ferry ride northwest of France lies a small island nation that once boasted that the sun never set on its empire. The United Kingdom of Great Britain and Northern Ireland is still a major world power, although it no longer controls a large colonial empire. The United Kingdom is also called Great Britain, and its citizens are considered British. The main island of the United Kingdom consists of three parts: England, which makes up most of the island; Scotland in the north; and Wales in the southwest. Northern Ireland makes up the northeast corner of a separate island across the Irish Sea to the west.

Surrounded by water, the British have always been drawn to the sea, and it has served them well. After they defeated the Spanish Armada in the late sixteenth century, the British began building their empire. They explored and colonized much of what is now the United States and Canada. They took control of much of Africa, including what is now Egypt, Sudan, Kenya, Uganda, Zimbabwe, Tanzania, Ivory Coast, Ghana, Nigeria, and South Africa. In Asia, the British controlled the Indian subcontinent, Burma, Singapore, Hong Kong, Malaysia, and Indonesia. They explored and populated Australia and New Zealand. Indeed, during its heyday in the nineteenth century, the sun truly did not set on the British Empire.

Great Britain sought colonies throughout the world to obtain raw materials. The British were the first masters of industry. Cotton, tea, sisal, coal, wood, iron, silk, coffee, cacao, rubber, copper, tin, and bauxite flowed into England. English industries made products with these raw materials. Then they exported their products all over the world at a great profit. Just a century ago, Britain was the wealthiest and most powerful nation on Earth.

Visual Aids

Besides the text, there are other parts to some reading material. There may be maps or graphs. Sometimes you will see illustrations or photos. These are all visual aids, or graphics. Visual aids use some form of picture to help readers understand information.

Check visual aids for titles, key words, and labels. Read the captions (labels or explanations) under photographs. Sometimes a visual aid is worth a thousand words.

■ PRACTICE 48: Visual Aids

The following passage has a visual aid: an illustration. After looking at the illustration, read the article. Then answer the questions.

Greek Style

The oldest style used in building Greek temples was the Doric style. It was a simple style of architecture, featuring columns that had no decoration at their tops. Before long, a second style started to be used. Architects used the Ionic style as early as the sixth century B.C.E. The Ionic style was more elegant, with columns topped by ram's horns. A third and later style was called Corinthian. The Corinthian was a fancier form of the Ionic. The tops of

Corinthian-style columns were decorated, too. They sported acanthus leaves. The Greeks did not build many temples with Corinthian-style columns. Sometimes the Greeks did not even use traditional columns to support temple roofs. They used statues instead.

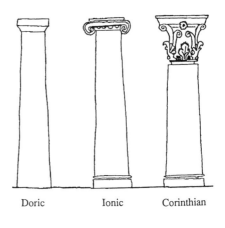

Doric   Ionic   Corinthian

1. Which style of Greek column is the fanciest?

   _____

2. Which style of Greek column is the simplest?

   _____

3. Did you understand the description of columns "topped by ram's horns" without the illustration? _____

THINK ABOUT IT

Some people find visual aids very helpful. Others prefer reading information in paragraph form.

Think about your own reading and learning style. For example, when you are going someplace new, do you prefer to look at a map? Or would you rather have the directions written out? On another sheet of paper, explain your preference.

UNIT 5 REVIEW

Scan the following paragraph. Then answer the questions. You may read the questions first.

Fashion played a part in spurring the exploration of North America. It may seem strange today that clothing would encourage people to explore a continent. But in the seventeenth, eighteenth, and nineteenth centuries, certain hats and coats were very popular in Europe. To make them, beaver fur was needed. The streams, creeks, and rivers flowing through America's rich forests were home to many of these animals. It was while hunting for beaver skins, or pelts, that English, French, Dutch, and Russian explorers mapped out the Great Lakes, the Northwest, Canada, and Alaska. They battled with one another and with American Indians over the land. Thousands of trappers searched deep into the forests for the valuable furs. The trappers brought their skins to trading posts such as Montreal, Quebec, Ottawa, Detroit, St. Paul, St. Louis, and Milwaukee. American Indians began trapping and trading beaver pelts, too.

1. What continent is discussed in the paragraph?_____
   _____

2. What were the explorers looking for? _____
   _____

3. Where did the explorers come from? _____
   _____

4. How did the fur trade affect American Indians? _____
   _____

UNIT 5 APPLICATION ACTIVITY
Scanning for News

Choose an interesting headline from a newspaper. Choose a key word or two from the headline. Write three questions based on the key word or words. Then scan the article and try to find the answer to each question.

Headline: _____

Key word(s): _____

Question: _____

_____

Answer: _____

_____

Question: _____

_____

Answer: _____

_____

Question: _____

_____

Answer: _____

_____

UNIT 6
Analyzing What You Read

LESSON 13: Fact and Opinion

 GOAL: To recognize fact and opinion in a reading passage

WORDS TO KNOW

fact   opinion

Identifying Fact and Opinion

To become a successful reader, you must be able to tell the difference between fact and opinion. If you cannot, you may accept someone else's beliefs as facts.

Any true detail is a *fact*. Facts can be proved to be true or false. For instance, the statement "This cake is chocolate with vanilla filling" can be checked by cutting into the cake and tasting it.

An opinion is a statement of the personal beliefs of the speaker or writer. An opinion can be argued. For example, the statement "This cake is delicious" is an opinion based on the speaker's preferences. Others may disagree.

The difference between fact and opinion is very important when reading newspapers, editorials, political writings, and advertisements. You must be able to tell fact from opinion in order to develop your own opinions and judgments.

Look at the pairs of sentences that appear on the next page.

Facts	Opinions
He was driving 65 miles per hour.	He was driving too fast.
Mike has a medical degree.	Mike is a good doctor.
This camera costs $50.	This camera is a good deal.
Monica spends a lot of time on her homework.	Monica deserves a good grade.
France has many rocky beaches.	The beaches in France are the best in the world.

TIP

Sometimes writers give you clues when they write opinions. Phrases such as *in my opinion, I think,* and *I believe* are all opinion signals.

Often, extreme adjectives also signal opinions. Words such as *amazing, fantastic, unbeatable, stupendous, wonderful,* and so on can be opinion signals.

■ PRACTICE 49: Identifying Fact and Opinion

Read each statement. Decide if each sentence gives a fact or an opinion. Write *fact* or *opinion* on the line.

1. Teresa was born June 7, 1992. _____

2. Tim is a hard worker. _____

3. Tim works 80 hours a week. _____

4. Two thousand people live in Milford. _____

5. Milford is a sleepy little town. _____

6. The teacher has an advanced degree. _____

7. He is an excellent teacher. _____

▮ PRACTICE 50: Recognizing Fact and Opinion

Read the following paragraph. Then read it again and circle the number of each sentence that gives an opinion.

(1) This set of knives has 21 pieces. (2) The knives are made of a hard stainless steel alloy. (3) They will not rust or corrode. (4) They also come with a lifetime warranty. (5) If you are not 100 percent satisfied, you can return them for your money back. (6) But surely you will be amazed at how easily they chop. (7) There is no better knife set on the market. (8) For a limited time, you can get the entire set for only $19.95. (9) You will never see such an incredible value again!

Now write the clues that told you a sentence contained an opinion.

_____

_____

_____

_____

_____

_____

_____

When is it all right to print or broadcast an opinion, and when should only facts be given?

In theory, journalism gives just facts. In reality, many newspapers or television news shows are seen as being for a particular side or another.

How does this "slant," or underlying opinion, affect the news you get? Read an article on the same event from two or three different newspapers. Or watch television news coverage of the same event on different stations. Do you get clues that the news is slanted one way or another? Write the results of your experiment below.

_____

_____

_____

_____

_____

_____

_____

_____

_____

LESSON 14: The Author's Purpose

 GOAL: To understand and recognize the author's purpose

WORDS TO KNOW

describe	explain	persuade or convince
entertain	inform	word choice

Identifying the Author's Purpose

People have many reasons for reading. They may be looking for information. They may want to understand something. They may just want to be entertained.

Just as people have different reasons for reading, writers have a variety of reasons for writing. Here are some of them:

Purposes for Writing

to describe—to create an image of something for the reader

to entertain—to write for the pleasure of the reader

to explain—to write so that the reader understands something

to inform—to give the reader information

to persuade or convince—to present arguments or information to lead the reader to agree with the writer

It is important to recognize the purpose behind what you read. Reading is a form of communication with a writer. If you don't know why the writer is telling you something, you may miss the point of the reading. And if you can figure out why a writer has written something, you will be alert for that person's opinions as well as facts.

What was the purpose of the paragraph about the knife set in the last lesson? It did describe the knives and inform you about them. But the overall purpose was to persuade you to buy them. The paragraph was an advertisement, an ad! The purpose of an ad is always to persuade you to do or to buy something.

Some people like to read and watch ads. Some ad campaigns become popular. Are there any ads that you enjoy? Why? Explain your answers on another sheet of paper.

■ PRACTICE 51: Identifying the Author's Purpose

Read the passage below. Think about the purpose of each paragraph. Then answer the questions.

Charlemagne was a famous king of the Middle Ages. He was strong and well-built. His neck was short and thick. His belly was a bit fat. The top of Charlemagne's head was round and, later in life, covered with snowy white hair. His eyes were large, and his nose was rather long. Whether standing or sitting, Charlemagne always looked dignified.

Charlemagne was an unusual man for his time. Most Germans were rough and unrefined. They fought constantly. They did not know how to read or write.

Unlike most of his German subjects, Charlemagne was educated. He was a fierce warrior, but also a wise ruler. He spread Christianity, education, and trade. Charlemagne's qualities helped shape the time in which he lived.

Charlemagne was a truly amazing military leader. He organized ragged German troops into a great army. He won many wars and conquered many people. He beat the Lombards in Italy in 774 C.E. He also fought against the Muslims in northern Spain. He beat the Bretons in England in 799 C.E. and defeated the Saxon tribes in 804 C.E. In the east, Charlemagne crushed the Avars and took over their lands. In 810 C.E. he conquered the Frisian Island off Holland and Denmark. Thus Charlemagne reunited the western Roman Empire.

1. What is the main purpose of the first paragraph about Charlemagne?
   a. to inform   b. to describe   c. to persuade

2. What is the main purpose of the second paragraph?
   a. to inform   b. to describe   c. to persuade

3. What is the purpose of the last paragraph?
   a. to inform   b. to describe   c. to persuade

4. List three opinions given in the article.

   _____

   _____

   _____

Nelly and Jared arrived late for a movie and missed the beginning. They did not enjoy the rest of the movie because they had trouble following the story. They didn't know who all the characters were. They didn't know why some things were happening.

Just like the beginning of a movie, the beginning of an article or essay often introduces the purpose for writing.

Identifying Writing Styles

When you read something, you want to know why the author has written it. You want to be able to tell fact from opinion. You may want to get certain information from the written text.

Part of understanding what you read is understanding what the author thinks of his or her subject. The writer does not always come out and state his or her feelings. But there are clues. You can tune in to the writer's style.

There are many writing styles. Here are a few:

descriptive—uses adjectives and images to describe something

humorous—uses humor to make the reader smile

informative—gives information

narrative—tells a story

persuasive—tries to convince you to agree with or do something

You probably noticed that some of the writing styles use the same words as author's purposes. But the two do not always match up. For example, a writer may want to inform people about a serious problem. The purpose is to inform. But she may decide to get your interest by telling a story about the problem. This is the narrative style. Or she may use humor to hook you, even though the subject is serious.

■ PRACTICE 52: Identifying Writing Styles

Read the following passage. Then answer the questions. Circle the letter of your answer.

"Sire, sire! The peasants are revolting!" cried the servant.

"Well, of course they're revolting," answered King Richard II. "They are peasants. They never bathe and they smell awful."

"No, sire. I mean they are rebelling, protesting, not following the rules. Their leader wishes to speak with you."

"Who is their leader?" demanded the king.

"Wat," replied the servant.

"Who is their leader?" repeated the king loudly.

"Wat is his name," the servant said.

"Yes!" said the king impatiently. "What is his name?"

"Wat, sire!" answered the servant.

"Are you growing deaf, boy? I asked his name!" the king shouted.

"That's what I'm trying to tell you," the servant replied. "Their leader's name is Wat. Wat Tyler!"

1. What is the writing style of this passage?
   a. informative **b.** descriptive **c.** humorous

2. What is the main idea of this passage?
   a. The servant is deaf.
   b. The king does not understand what the servant is trying to tell him.
   c. Wat Tyler is leading a peasant's revolt.

3. What is the purpose of this passage?
   a. to inform
   b. to entertain
   c. to persuade or convince

THINK ABOUT IT

The passage about the servant telling the king about Wat Tyler describes a moment in history. Think about the history textbooks you have read. Why might an author use some humor in an essay about history? Write your ideas on a separate sheet of paper.

Word Choice

Writers work with words. They use time words to tell you about sequence. They use context clues to help you figure out new words. They use a variety of words to keep their writing interesting.

Writers choose particular words to make their point. Sometimes, there are synonyms to choose from. The words a writer uses can express shades of meaning. They can also express strong feeling. The particular words a writer uses is his or her word choice. The overall feeling you get from a piece of writing is created, in part, by word choice.

Authors have a purpose for everything they write. They choose a style to fit that purpose. Their word choice can clue you in to their opinion about their subject.

Word choice is a persuasive tool. Writers use words that will convince you to agree with them in their opinion of their subject. Read the following descriptions:

A fresh breeze swirled through the trees. The rustling leaves meant there were woodland animals nearby. The excited bird calls from above told us our winged friends had noticed us.

A strong wind blew through the trees. The stirred-up leaves meant there were wild creatures nearby. The loud cries from above told us the birds knew we were there.

The paragraphs describe the same thing: a windy day in the woods. But the word choice is quite different. The first paragraph uses positive, upbeat words. The feeling the reader gets is of a happy, pleasant scene. The second paragraph uses rather negative words. The reader feels that the scene is rather frightening.

■ PRACTICE 53: Word Choice

Read the following paragraphs about Charlemagne. (You have seen them before.) Think about the author's opinion of the subject. Then answer the questions.

Charlemagne was a famous king of the Middle Ages. He was strong and well-built. His neck was short and thick.

His belly was a bit fat. The top of Charlemagne's head was round and, later in life, covered with snowy white hair. His eyes were large, and his nose was rather long. Whether standing or sitting, Charlemagne always looked dignified.

Charlemagne was an unusual man for his time. Most Germans were rough and unrefined. They fought constantly. They did not know how to read or write. Unlike most of his German subjects, Charlemagne was educated. He was a fierce warrior, but also a wise ruler. He spread Christianity, education, and trade. Charlemagne's qualities helped shape the time in which he lived.

Charlemagne was a truly amazing military leader. He organized ragged German troops into a great army. He won many wars and conquered many people. He beat the Lombards in Italy in 774 C.E. He also fought against the Muslims in northern Spain. He beat the Bretons in England in 799 C.E. and defeated the Saxon tribes in 804 C.E. In the east, Charlemagne crushed the Avars and took over their lands. In 810 C.E., he conquered the Frisian Island off Holland and Denmark. Thus Charlemagne reunited the western Roman Empire.

1. What is the overall feeling of this article?
   a. respectful   b. disgusted   c. fearful

2. What is the author's overall opinion of Charlemagne?
   a. He was a great man.
   b. He was unattractive.
   c. He was always looking for a fight.

3. The author sums up Charlemagne's appearance with the word *dignified.* Reread the first paragraph. If the author did not admire Charlemagne, what other word might he have used in place of *dignified?*

_____

4. "Thus Charlemagne reunited the western Roman Empire." What is the feeling of this sentence?

   a. positive   **b.** negative

5. Imagine this was the last sentence of the article: "Thus Charlemagne forced the western Roman Empire to reunite." What would the feeling be with the new word choice?

   a. positive   **b.** negative

UNIT 6 REVIEW

Read the paragraph. Then answer the questions.

In 1944, a tragedy in Hartford, Connecticut, brought about change in the circus world. A great fire ripped through the Ringling Bros. and Barnum & Bailey® circus during a summer performance. The big-top tent measured 520 feet long and weighed over 19 tons. It was the largest piece of canvas in the world. The tent had been treated with a solution to make it waterproof. No one realized it at the time, but the solution was flammable. Even though the circus performers worked hard to get the spectators out, many died. As a result of the tragedy, "the greatest show on earth" and other circuses perform under different materials today.

1. Which of the following is a fact?
   a. The big-top tent measured 520 feet long and weighed over 19 tons.
   b. The circus performers worked hard to get the spectators out.
   c. The Ringling Bros. and Barnum & Bailey® circus is the greatest show on earth.

2. Which of the following is an opinion?
   a. The big-top tent measured 520 feet long and weighed over 19 tons.
   b. A fire ripped through the Ringling Bros. and Barnum & Bailey® circus during a summer performance.
   c. The Ringling Bros. and Barnum & Bailey® circus is the greatest show on earth.

3. What is the author's purpose in writing this paragraph?
   a. to persuade   b. to inform   c. to entertain

UNIT 6 APPLICATION ACTIVITY
Facts and Opinions in Editorials

Turn to the editorial section of a newspaper. In this section, you will find articles that give the writer's opinion as well as facts.

Choose an article and read it. On a separate sheet of paper, list the opinions in one column and facts in a second column. Then, using only the facts you listed, rewrite the article as a factual article. Use a separate sheet of paper.

UNIT 7

Remembering What You Read

LESSON 15: Underlining

GOAL: To learn to use underlining to remember important information in a reading passage

WORD TO KNOW

underlining

Reading involves a lot of brain power. When you read, you use many skills to understand words, paragraphs, and whole passages. You have learned to find main ideas, draw conclusions, and understand sequence. You can analyze a piece of writing for the author's purpose and style. This helps you to be aware of what is fact and what is opinion.

After all that thought, you do not want to forget what you have read!

When you scan a passage, you look for key words. You do not read every word. When you read closely, you also look for key words and sentences. But you look for them while you are reading the whole passage.

Underlining

One way to keep track of important words and sentences is to underline them while you are reading. (You may prefer highlighting the information with a bright highlighting marker.) With underlining, you are pointing out important information to yourself.

Read the following paragraphs carefully. Pay attention to the words that have been underlined by a careful reader. Then use the underlined words to help you answer the questions.

Architecture is the art and science of building. During the Golden Age in Athens, it was both an art and a science. Architects in ancient Greece constructed some of the most beautiful buildings in the world. The Parthenon, a famous temple, has always been considered a work of art. It was also considered a work of science when it was built.

The Parthenon's architects knew that the human eye can play tricks. It can look at something that is straight and see it as curved—and the other way around. The architects did not want the Parthenon to look crooked. To avoid this, they found a way of fooling the eye. Instead of making the Parthenon's base straight, they made it curved. The base curves slightly upward in the center. It looks as though it is even, but it is not. The Parthenon's architects also made the columns bulge near their centers. This made them appear perfectly straight!

1. Architecture is both
    a. nature and technology.
    b. art and science.
    c. ancient and modern.

2. When were many beautiful Greek buildings built?
    a. during the Bronze Age of Athens
    b. during the Silver Age of Athens
    c. during the Golden Age of Athens

3. What famous building does this article describe?
    a. the Parthenon   b. the Coliseum   c. the Museum

4. What did the architects think about when they designed the temple?

    a. the light   **b.** the weather   **c.** the human eye

5. Why did the architects put bulges in the columns?

    a. to make them appear straight

    b. to make them appear taller

    c. to make them appear wider

How did you do? When you underline or highlight important words, you make it easy to review what you have read. (The answers are 1. b, 2. c, 3. a, 4. c, 5. a.)

PRACTICE 54: Underlining

Read the following paragraph carefully. Underline the important information. Then answer the questions.

Hellenistic Mathematics

During the Hellenistic (ancient Greek) period, there was a golden age of science. Many advances were made in mathematics. Euclid summarized the basics of geometry. He wrote a book. That book was used for 2,000 years to teach geometry. Archimedes of Syracuse created a new branch of mathematics. He was also a brilliant engineer. He invented levers and pulleys. He invented an endless screw, too. It is still used to lift water from one level to another.

1. What was in Euclid's book?_____

2. What did Archimedes invent?_____

3. What does Archimedes' screw do?_____

LESSON 16: Summarizing

 GOAL: To learn to summarize to remember information in a reading passage

WORDS TO KNOW

outline   summary

Summarizing: The Outline

A **summary** is a brief description of the main ideas of a passage. You have already practiced summarizing, or putting into a few words, the main idea of a paragraph in a title.

One form of summary is an **outline.** An outline lists facts or ideas in order of importance. Outlining as you read will help you remember facts and ideas.

An outline follows this form:

Title

  A. (main idea)

     1. (supporting detail)

       a. (more detail)

       b. (more detail)

     2. (supporting detail)

     3. (supporting detail)

  B. (main idea)

     1. (supporting detail)

     2. (supporting detail)

     3. (supporting detail)

Of course, you may need to add more lines, depending on your passage.

Read the following paragraph. The important information has been underlined.

Hellenistic Astronomy

Many advances were made in astronomy during the Hellenistic period. <u>Aristarchus</u> of Samos suggested that the <u>earth moved in a circle around the sun</u>. He also <u>tried to measure the distance of the moon and the sun from the earth</u>. Eratosthenes of Cyrene was a friend of Archimedes'. <u>Eratosthenes observed the location of the sun in the sky</u>. He observed it from different places. He found that its location in the sky changed. Eratosthenes <u>concluded that the earth was curved</u>. He wanted to know the <u>distance around the middle of the earth</u>. Using <u>geometry</u>, he came up with an answer. He <u>calculated that the distance</u> around the middle of the earth was 25,000 miles. He was <u>very close</u> to being correct.

Underlining alone helps you remember and review what you have read. Taking underlining a step further can be even more helpful. You can use your underlining to summarize a passage in an outline. Let's try it.

Hellenistic Astronomy

A. Aristarchus
   1. suggested the earth moved around the sun
   2. tried to measure (do not know if successful):
     a. distance of moon from the earth
     b. distance of the sun from the earth

B. Eratosthenes
1. concluded the earth was curved
   a. observed sun in sky from different places
   b. noticed location changed
2. wanted to know distance around middle of the earth
   a. used geometry to calculate
   b. came close to correct answer

■ PRACTICE 55: Summarizing: The Outline

Read the following passage carefully. (You have seen it before.) Underline important information. Use this information to create an outline. Then answer the questions using the outline you have completed.

Greek Style

The oldest style used in building Greek temples was the Doric style. It was a simple style of architecture, featuring columns that had no decoration at their tops. Before long, a second style started to be used. Architects used the Ionic style as early as the sixth century B.C.E. The Ionic style was more elegant, with columns topped by ram's horns. A third and later style was called Corinthian. The Corinthian was a fancier form of the Ionic. The tops of Corinthian-style columns were decorated, too. They sported acanthus leaves. The Greeks did not build many temples with Corinthian-style columns. Sometimes the Greeks did not even use traditional columns to support temple roofs. They used statues instead.

Complete the outline that has been started below.

Greek Style

A. Doric
   1. oldest style for temples
   2. columns had no decoration

1. What are the three types of Greek styles discussed?

   _____

2. Which of these is the oldest style? _____

3. What kind of decoration do Corinthian-style columns have?

   _____

Summarizing: Paragraph Form

An outline is a great memory and review tool. Some people like the visual format of lists in order of importance.

Other people prefer to read information in paragraph form. Writing a summary in a paragraph is another way to help you remember what you have read.

Look at this example of a summary in paragraph form. It is based on the article "Greek Style."

> The Doric style is the oldest style of Greek temples. Doric-style columns have no decoration. The next style is the Ionic. This is fancier, with ram's horns decorations. A later style, not used much, is the Corinthian. The columns had acanthus leaves as decoration.

This summary paragraph covers all the important information. It is a shorter, more condensed form of the original article.

■ PRACTICE 56: Summarizing: Paragraph Form

Read the following passage. Underline important information. Use this to write a summary paragraph. Then answer the questions.

> Elijah McCoy was very interested in mechanical engineering. He tried to find a job in which he could develop his interests and talents. But it was the mid-nineteenth century, and he was a young African American. He had to settle for a position as a coal shoveler for the railroads.
>
> While performing his job, he noticed how inefficient trains were. For one thing, they had to stop often for lubrication (to be oiled). McCoy figured out a way for the locomotive to be lubricated while in motion, thus making

railroad travel much more efficient. This invention led to many others.

McCoy became so successful inventing useful devices for the railroad that whenever people were in the market for railroad equipment, they always made sure they got "the real McCoy."

Summary paragraph:

_____

_____

_____

_____

1. Why did McCoy take a job as a coal shoveler? _____

   _____

2. What was McCoy's first invention for railroads?_____

   _____

3. What does "the real McCoy" mean? _____

   _____

UNIT 7 REVIEW

Read the following paragraphs. Underline important information as you read. You may want to make an outline on another sheet of paper. You may want to summarize the information in a paragraph. Then answer the questions.

An unlikely hero came to the world's attention in 1995. One woman who wanted to help poor children attend college donated $150,000 to the University of Southern Mississippi.

Certainly, it is an act of selflessness when anyone helps others. When that person turns out to be someone whose only source of income was doing other people's laundry, the gift is even more extraordinary.

This woman was Oseola McCarty. She was 86 years old when she created her scholarship. Her remarkable story began when she had to quit school after the sixth grade. Her aunt, who had worked with McCarty's mother and another aunt, fell ill. Oseola was needed to help out with the washing and ironing the family did to earn money.

Those were the days before automatic washers and dryers. McCarty had to haul water from the fire hydrant. Then she boiled the water in a large pot. Finally, she scrubbed the clothes on a washboard and hung them to dry on a clothesline. Her workdays began at sunrise and continued until the job was finished. This work was physically demanding, but it made McCarty feel proud.

To her family, friends, and neighbors, McCarty was always known as shy and hardworking. She began saving money as a child, and her savings grew. When she began to think about what to do with her savings when she was gone, she decided to start the scholarship. It is the single largest gift the University of Southern Mississippi has ever received from an African American.

Ms. McCarty did not want attention for her gift. She wanted to stay anonymous, or unknown. But because of her amazing story, she was asked to appear on many television shows. She even met President Clinton at the White House. In 1999, Ms. McCarty died of cancer. She will be remembered for her philosophy of helping others: "I can't do everything. But I can do something to help somebody. And what I can do I will do. I wish I could do more."

1. What was Oseola McCarty's gift? _____

_____

2. What had Ms. McCarty's job been? _____

_____

3. How much education had she had? _____

_____

4. When did Oseola McCarty die? _____

UNIT 7 APPLICATION ACTIVITY
Remembering Facts for Class

Get a jump on your reading for another class. Read a chapter or section carefully. Underline as you go. Use this information to make an outline or write a summary on a separate sheet of paper. When the time comes for a test, you will have a useful review tool!

APPENDIXES

A. Prefixes

Prefix	Meaning	Prefix	Meaning
bi-	two	mis-	not, opposite of
de-	not, opposite of	non-	not, opposite of
dis-	not, opposite of	post-	after
ex-	former, formerly, no longer	pre-	before
extra-	beyond	re-	again
il-	not, opposite of	semi-	half
im-	not, opposite of	sub-	below, under
in-	not, opposite of	super-	over, above
inter-	between	trans-	across
intra-	within	tri-	three
ir-	not, opposite of	un-	not, opposite of
mal-	bad	uni-	one

B. Suffixes

Suffix	Meaning	Suffix	Meaning
-able	capable of being	-ify	to make; to cause to be; to become
-al	like; suitable for		
-an	follower; thing; pertaining to	-ion	being; the result of
		-ish	similar to
-ance	state of being	-ist	one who
-ant	thing; one who	-ize	to make; to cause to be; to become
-ation	being; the result of		
-en	to make; to cause to be; to become	-less	without
		-ly	pertaining to; in the manner of
-ence	state; fact; quality		
-ent	to form	-ment	a means; product; act; state
-er	doer; thing; to do		
-ful	full of	-ness	state; condition
-hood	state; condition	-or	person; thing that
		-ous	characterized by; having quality of
-ian	related to; one that is		
		-ship	state; condition
-ible	capable of being	-tion	being; the result of
-ic	like; having the nature of	-y	marked by; having
-ical	connected with		

C. Roots

Root	Meaning
bi, bio	life
cede, ceed, cess	go; yield
cred	believe
dic, dict	say
duce, duct	lead
fact, fect, feit, fict	make; do
fer	carry
ject	throw
junct	join
mis, mit	send
pone, pose	place, put
port	carry
scrib, scrip	write
secu, sequ	follow
vene, vent	come
vers, vert	turn
voc, voke	call

GLOSSARY

alphabetical order (al-fuh-BE-ti-kul OR-dur) words arranged starting with the letter *a* and ending with the letter *z*

antonym (AN-tuh-nim) a word that means the opposite of another word

base word (BAYS WURD) a word that forms the main part of a longer word

bold type (BOHLD TYPE) words that are darker than other words to help you find them more easily

cause (KOZ) something that makes another thing happen

compare (kum-PAYR) to show how two or more things are alike

compound word (COM-pownd WURD) a word made up of two base words put together

conclusion (kun-KLOO-zhun) the end, as of a book or play

context (KON-tekst) the information surrounding a word

contrast (kun-TRAST) to show how two or more things are different

definition (de-fuh-NI-shun) the meaning of a word

describe (de-SKRYB) to write with the purpose of giving specific details about something

description (di-SKRIP-shun) the details of an object

detail (dee-TAYL) a small part of a whole; item

dictionary (DIK-shuh-ner-ee) a reference tool for words that shows how to pronounce words, their correct spellings, the syllables of the words, their origins, and their definitions

effect (ee-FEKT) what happens as a result of a cause

entertain (en-tur-TAYN) to write with the purpose of amusing the audience

entry (EN-tree) each word defined in a dictionary

example (ig-ZAM-pul) something that is chosen or studied because it is like other things of the same kind

explain (ik-SPLAYN) to write with the purpose of making something clear

explanation (ek-spluh-NAY-shun) something that makes something else clear or understandable

fact (FAKT) a detail that can be proved true

future tense (FYOO-chur TENS) verb tense that indicates that something will happen or is about to happen

generalize (JEN-ruh-lyz) to make a broad statement based on specific details

graphics (GRA-fiks) illustrations or photos within the text

guide words (GYD WURDZ) the first and last words on each page of the dictionary that are printed at the top of the page

---

PRONUNCIATION KEY

CAPITAL LETTERS show the stressed syllables.

a	as in mat	f	as in fit
ay	as in day, say	g	as in go
ch	as in chew	i	as in sit
e	as in bed	j	as in job, gem
ee	as in even, easy, need	k	as in cool, key

headings (HED-ingz) words used to divide text into sections

headlines (HED-lynz) words at the top of a newspaper article

inform (in-FORM) to write with the purpose of teaching the audience

key words (KEE WURDZ) words that are related to what you want to find out

main idea (MAYN y-DEE-uh) the single idea discussed in a piece of writing

opinion (uh-PIN-yun) a statement of personal belief that can be argued

outline (OWT-lyn) a list of facts or ideas in order of importance

paragraph (PAR-uh-graf) a group of sentences that discuss a single idea

past perfect tense (PAST PUR-fikt TENS) a verb tense that indicates a past action came before another past action

past tense (PAST TENS) a verb tense that indicates something happened in the past

persuade or convince (pur-SWAYD/kun-VINS) to write with the purpose of influencing the audience

---

PRONUNCIATION KEY

g	as in running	oo	as in too
	as in cot, father	u	as in but, some
h	as in go, note	uh	as in about, taken, lemon, pencil
h	as in shy	ur	as in term
h	as in thin	y	as in line, fly
		zh	as in vision, measure

prefix (PREE-fiks) a word part added to the beginning of a word to make a new word

present tense (PRE-zunt TENS) verb tense that indicates something is happening right now or happens regularly

restatement (ree-STAYT-munt) stating a main point for a second time

root (ROOT) a type of word part; a base that is not a stand-alone word itself

scan (SKAN) to briefly look for information without reading every word

scanning (SKAN-ing) quickly looking for specific information without reading every word

sequence (SEE-kwuns) the order in which things happen

suffix (SUH-fiks) a word part that is added to the end of a word to make a new word

summarizing (SUH-muh-ryz-ing) summing up the main ideas of a passage

summary (SUH-muh-ree) a brief description of the main ideas of a passage

---

PRONUNCIATION KEY

a	as in m**a**t	f	as in **f**it
ay	as in d**ay**, s**ay**	g	as in **g**o
ch	as in **ch**ew	i	as in s**i**t
e	as in b**e**d	j	as in **j**ob, **g**em
ee	as in **e**ven, **ea**sy, n**ee**d	k	as in **c**ool, **k**ey

synonym (SI-nuh-nim) a word that means almost the same thing as another word

topic sentence (TO-pik SEN-tuns) the sentence that states the main idea

underlining (UN-dur-lyn-ing) writing lines under important words to keep track of information

verb tenses (VURB TEN-sez) forms of verbs that indicate when the action happened

visual aids (VI-zhuh-wul AYDZ) graphs, maps, illustrations, or photos within the text

word choice (WURD CHOYS) the particular words an author uses

PRONUNCIATION KEY

ng	as in running	oo	as in too
	as in cot, father	u	as in but, some
oh	as in go, note	uh	as in about, taken, lemon, pencil
sh	as in shy	ur	as in term
th	as in thin	y	as in line, fly
		zh	as in vision, measure

INDEX

ditorials, 120
ffect, 74
ntertaining, 111
ntry, 46
    looking for dictionary, 46–48
vidence, collecting, 66
xamples, as context clues, 37
xplanation, 111
    as context clue, 37

acts
    being alert for, 112
    for class, remembering, 133
    definition of, 107
    difference between
    opinions and, 107
    in editorials, 120
    examples of, 108
    identifying, 107–109
    in journalism, 110
    outlining, to help remember, 126
    recognizing, 109
lowcharts, 75
uture tense, 77

eneralizing, 67–69
raphic organizers, 73
raphics, 100
raphs, 100
uide words, 46

eadings, 95
eadlines, newspaper, 59, 95
    choosing key words in, 103

llustrations, 100
nforming, 111

key words, 91
    called out for readers, 95
    checking visual aids for, 100
    in newspaper headlines, 103
    scanning for, 91–95

labels, on visual aids, 100

main ideas, 55
    pinpointing, 60
maps, 100

newspapers
    editorials, 120
    headlines, 59, 95, 103
    looking for clues for "slant" in, 110
noun(s)
    dictionary abbreviation for, 50
    suffixes, 18–19

opinions
    being alert for, 112
    definition of, 107
    difference between facts and, 107
    in editorials, 120
    examples of, 108
    identifying, 107–109
    recognizing, 109
    slanting, in news, 110
outlines, 126
    form of, 126

paragraphs, 55
    preference for, as opposed
    to visual aids, 101
    questions in, 60–61
    summarizing, in titles, 57
    topic sentences in, 98
    writing summary in, 129–131

summarizing
  in newspapers, 59
  the outline, 126–129
  paragraph form of, 129–131
  paragraphs, as titles, 57
summary, 126
synonyms, 29–31
  being careful when choosing, 29
  as context clues, 37
  remembering difference between
    antonyms and, 32
  use of, by writers, 116

tests, reviewing for, 92
text elements, 95–96
time
  clues, 80, 81
  meanings, prefixes with, 8–9
  specific words for, 82–83
  verb tenses, to place events in, 80
  words, to tell about sequence, 116
titles
  checking visual aids for, 100
  in newspapers, 59
  summarizing paragraphs in, 57
topic sentences, 55
  recognizing, 55–56
  scanning for, 98

underlining, 123–125

Venn diagrams, 73
verb(s). See also verb tenses
  in dictionaries, 46–47
  dictionary abbreviation for, 50
  suffixes, 15–16
verb tenses
  future tense, 77
  identifying, 77

past perfect tense, 78
past tense, 77
to place events in time, 80
present tense, 77
using, to recognize sequence, 79
visual aids, 100–101
vocabulary
  journal, keeping, 47
  use of specialized, 30
  using synonyms and antonyms
    to build, 29–33

word choice, 116–117
  importance of, 117
words
  action, 15. See also verb(s)
  base, 3, 5–6
    finding, 6
  compound, 3–4
    meanings of, 4–5
  examples of specific time, 82
  finding, in dictionary, 45
  keeping track of
    important, 123–125
  recognizing compare and
    contrast, 70–71
  sequence, 87
  that signal cause and effect, 74
  time, used by writers, 116
  understanding meanings of,
    from context, 34–35
  writers' choice of, 116–117
writing
  importance of word
    choice in, 116–117
  purposes for, 111–112
  styles, identifying, 114–115